Thematic Unit

World War II

Written by Julie R. Strathman

Teacher Created Materials, Inc.

P.O. Box 1214

Huntington Beach, CA 92647

©*1994 Teacher Created Materials, Inc.*

Made in U.S.A.

ISBN 1-55734-581-3

Illustrations by

Keith Vasconcelles

Cover Art by

Kathy Bruce

Table of Contents

Introduction

World War II contains a comprehensive whole language, thematic unit. Its 80 reproducible pages are filled with a wide variety of lesson ideas designed for use with intermediate and junior high school students. At its core are three high-quality reading selections, *V Is for Victory*, *Number the Stars*, and *Sadako and the Thousand Paper Cranes*.

There are activities for each selection which set the stage for reading, encourage the enjoyment of the book, and extend the concepts. Activities are also provided that integrate the curriculum areas of language arts (including writing and research skills), math, science, social studies, art, music, and life skills. Many of these activities are conducive to the use of cooperative learning groups.

One or all of the books may be covered in this unit. They were selected with the distinct purpose of allowing students to analyze the effects of WW II from different perspectives. Students are encouraged to view the events of WW II as they affected the home front, as well as through the eyes of Jewish families living in Denmark and Japanese families living in Hiroshima, Japan. Higher level critical-thinking skills are developed as students examine a historical event from different viewpoints. The activities in this unit are designed to help students realize that WW II was not only a tumultuous period for Americans but also for people of other cultures in countries around the world.

Unit management tools include time saving suggestions, such as patterns for bulletin boards and learning centers. The activities allow students to synthesize their knowledge and make the events of WW II come to life.

This thematic unit includes:

- ¤ **literature selections**—summaries of three books with related lessons that cross the curriculum

- ¤ **planning guides**—suggestions for sequencing lessons of the unit

- ¤ **poetry**—suggested lessons that enable students to experience and write a type of poetry that comes from the Japanese culture

- ¤ **writing ideas**—daily writing suggestions and activities that cross the curriculum, including Big Books and Picture Books

- ¤ **bulletin boards**—suggestions and plans for content related and interactive bulletin boards

- ¤ **home/school connections**—for extending the unit to the student's home

- ¤ **curriculum connections**—in language arts, math, science, social studies, art, music, and life skills

- ¤ **group projects**—to foster cooperative learning

- ¤ **culminating activities**—which require students to synthesize their learning and participate in activities that can be shared with others

- ¤ **portfolio assessment form**—to record the student's performance during this unit

- ¤ **a bibliography**—suggesting additional literature and nonfiction books relating to this unit

To keep this valuable resource intact so that it can be used year after year, you may wish to punch holes in the pages and store them in a three-ring binder.

Introduction *(cont.)*

Why Whole Language?

A whole language approach involves children in using all modes of communication: reading, writing, listening, observing, illustrating, experiencing, and doing. Communication skills are interconnected and integrated into lessons that emphasize the whole of language rather than isolating its parts. The lessons revolve around selected literature. Reading is not taught as a separate subject from writing and spelling, for example. A child reads, writes, speaks, listens, and thinks in response to a literature experience introduced by the teacher. In this way, language skills grow naturally, stimulated by involvement and interest in the topic at hand.

Why Thematic Planning?

One very useful tool for implementing an integrated whole language program is thematic planning. By choosing a theme with correlating literature selections for a unit of study, a teacher can plan activities throughout the day that lead to a cohesive, in-depth study of the topic. Students will be practicing and applying their skills in meaningful contexts. Consequently, they will tend to learn and retain more. Both teachers and students will be freed from a day that is broken into unrelated segments of isolated drill and practice.

Why Cooperative Learning?

Besides academic skills and content, students need to learn social skills. No longer can this area of development be taken for granted. Students must learn to work cooperatively in groups in order to function well in modern society. Group activities should be a regular part of school life and teachers should consciously include social objectives as well as academic objectives in their planning. The teacher should clarify and monitor the qualities of good group interaction, just as he/she would clarify and monitor the academic goals of the project.

Why Big Books?

An excellent cooperative, whole language activity is the production of Big Books. Groups of students or the whole class, can apply their language skills, content knowledge, and creativity to produce a Big Book that can become a part of the classroom library to be read and reread. These books make excellent culminating projects for sharing beyond the classroom with parents, librarians, and others. Big Books can be produced in many ways, and this thematic unit book includes directions for several methods you may choose.

V Is for Victory

by Sylvia Whitman

Summary

This recently published, nonfiction book by Sylvia Whitman addresses many of the issues facing Americans on the home front during World War II. The text is written with the distinct purpose of explaining to readers how the events of WW II affected the life of every single American. War-time photographs and direct quotations from people who survived the war years add to the book's authenticity. Focusing on events, from the bombing of Pearl Harbor to the surrendering of Germany and Japan, **V Is for Victory** *not only provides factual information but also probes into the feelings of the American public. Several other aspects of the war on the home front are discussed, such as civil defense, Japanese relocation, rationing, propaganda, censorship, and the transition period for returning American veterans.*

V Is for Victory is an invaluable reference tool for a thematic unit on WW II or any lesson dealing with the hardships of war. Each section of the book should be correlated with the specific issues being addressed in the classroom. The sample lesson plan outlined below covers many of the main aspects of the home front during WW II, but these lessons should be adapted to meet the curriculum and individual needs of your class.

Sample Plan

Lesson 1

- Introduce the WW II time period (page 6).

- Read pages 6-14 of *V Is for Victory.*

- Answer questions about Pearl Harbor (page 11).

- Construct WW II diaries (pages 40-41), and write about the topic for Lesson 1 (page 42).

- Survey adults who were alive in the 1940's to find out what they were doing when they heard about the bombing of Pearl Harbor.

Lesson 2

- Read pages 15-17 and page 61.

- Write about the diary topic for Lesson 2 (page 42).

- Discuss the plight of the Japanese Americans (page 65).

Lesson 3

- Read pages 18-29.

- Write about the diary topic for Lesson 3 (pages 40-42).

- Discuss the meaning of the popular wartime slogan "Soldiers Without Guns."

- Discuss the role of women (page 12).

Lesson 4

- Read pages 30-41.

- Write about the diary topic for Lesson 4 (page 42).

- Complete the rationing activities (pages 49-51).

- Complete the recycling activities (pages 66-67).

V Is for Victory

Sample Plan (cont.)

Lesson 5

- Read pages 42-51.
- Write about the diary topic for Lesson 5 (page 42).
- Make a bar graph to show military deaths (pages 13-14).
- Research to compare the number of American casualties during WW II with those of previous wars. Use this data as a page in a Big Book (pages 70-71) or for a large bar graph in the Clouds of War Learning Center (page 72).
- Discuss the development of the atomic bomb (pages 52-55).

Lesson 6

- Read pages 52-63.
- Write about the diary topic for Lesson 6 (page 42).
- Discuss the WW II slogan "Ac-cent-chu-ate the Positive."
- Design a poster promoting patriotism (page 61).

Lesson 7

- Read pages 64-75.
- Write about the diary topic for Lesson 7 (page 42).
- Explore cause and effect (page 15).
- Complete a crossword puzzle (page 16).
- Create a time line (page 56).

Overview of Activities

SETTING THE STAGE

1. Introduce students to the political climate of the world prior to and during World War II. The Holocaust (pages 22-23) provides background information. Use World War II Vocabulary (page 43) as a resource, as well.

2. On a world map, have students locate the Axis countries: Japan, Italy, and Germany. Use A Changing Germany (pages 59-60) to help them fully grasp the volatile situation in Europe at this time.

3. To foster positive home/school communication, send home the parent letter (page 76) when introducing this unit of study. This letter also invites parents to help gather materials for the Clouds of War Learning Center (page 72).

4. Set up the Clouds of War Learning Center and appropriate bulletin boards (pages 72-74).

5. Have students construct World War II Diaries for the daily writing activities as they begin the task of viewing the events of WW II from three different perspectives (pages 40-41).

6. Introduce the unit using the picture books, *When Mama Retires* and *Don't You Know There's a War On?* (pages 8-9 and bibliography, page 78). Discuss with students the task of writing their own picture book of WW II on the home front (pages 9-10). This project should be used throughout the unit as students gather information and complete the writing and publishing process. These picture books may be published by individual students or by cooperative learning groups. After the books are completed, they should be placed in the Clouds of War Learning Center.

Overview of Activities *(cont.)*

ENJOYING THE BOOK

1. For the duration of this thematic unit on World War II, transform your classroom into a newspaper publishing company. Using the events of WW II as prompts for writing activities, have students create a newspaper (pages 44-45).

2. Have students research or discuss critical-thinking questions about WW II (page 11).

3. Have students complete the Let's Play Ball! worksheet (page 58). Extend this activity by having them locate information about other sports in which women now participate. Have them compare salaries and news coverage of professional female athletes to that of their male counterparts. Ask which sports are still considered off-limits for women. Have students make a chart in which they list the names of all the professional female and male athletes that they know. Before beginning, have students predict which list will be longer. After completing the chart, have them count to see if their prediction was correct.

4. Heighten student interest by having them complete the activities related to popular music during WW II (pages 63-64). Ask them to explore the mood of the country by listening to the same songs people heard on the radio during the war. Obtain a copy of the *Stage Door Canteen* which has over 40 original versions of songs that were popular during WW II (bibliography, page 78). Ask students to compare this music to that which is on the radio today.

5. Provide the opportunity for students to write their own songs about WW II, patriotism, or world peace (page 64). These songs may be performed at "The Spirit of America" Day (page 68). Students may be assigned to write their lyrics as an individual activity or as a group project.

6. Introduce the class writing project, The Long Road to Peace (pages 70-71). In this activity students make a class Big Book. Provide the materials needed to complete this project in the Clouds of War Learning Center (page 72). The pages describing this project give several variations so that it may be adapted to different ability levels.

EXTENDING THE BOOK

1. After introducing information about women entering the work force as symbolized by "Rosie the Riveter" (page 12), have students research the women's rights movement, beginning with World War II through the present. Have students use this information to create a time line. Ask for the names of people who played important roles in women's struggle for equality. Discuss with the class whether they believe today's women and men have equal rights.

2. Design a World News Update bulletin board (pages 23-24). Display summaries that students have written using newspaper articles about oppression and persecution in current world events. On the world map, ask them to locate and label the places described in their summaries.

3. Implement the Heroes on the Home Front research project (page 57) anytime during the WW II unit. Display the completed projects in the Clouds of War Learning Center (page 72).

4. Have students plan their celebration for "The Spirit of America" Day, using the activities which are correlated with the WW II thematic unit (page 68) and the invitation for special guests (page 69). Adapt this celebration to meet the needs of your class.

5. Have students make a pamphlet for *V Is for Victory* (page 75).

Picture This

Most people, regardless of their age, enjoy a creatively illustrated and well-written picture book. Two recently published picture books, *Don't You Know There's a War On?* by James Stevenson and *When Mama Retires* by Karen Ackerman are excellent examples of how authors can explain a complex subject, such as World War II, and concisely reflect the mood of the times.

Read More About It!

Don't You Know There's a War On? simply and candidly describes life in the U.S. during World War II through the eyes of a ten-year-old boy. The tone of the text and illustrations ranges from serious to humorous. The book describes different facets of life on the home front including victory gardens, rationing, spies, and even SPAM (meat in a can). The very first sentence of the book, "In 1942 there was a war....", indicates that the author has an important message to tell.

When Mama Retires describes how the life of a typical American family changes when the father goes overseas to fight in World War II. The mother in the story ponders the question of whether she should continue her housekeeping duties or join the ranks of women who are helping the war effort by working in factories. If she takes a factory job, her three young sons will have to help out by doing many of the housekeeping chores. After following their mother around the house for just one day, the boys hope they will be ready to take over "when mama retires."

Use *Don't You Know There's a War On?* and *When Mama Retires* for the activities on page 9.

Picture Book Activities

Use the two picture books, *Don't You Know There's a War On?* and *When Mama Retires*, that are summarized on page 8 for the following activities. You may also wish to include additional picture books about World War II for some or all of these activities.

1. Read aloud these two picture books to students when introducing the World War II unit and as a catalyst for discussion. Have students imagine what it was like to be alive during the war. Ask them what they would have done to help the war effort.

2. Have students work in cooperative learning groups to write scripts by adapting the text of these picture books so that they can be performed as plays for other classes. Students may wish to create some simple props for their plays.

3. Have students read aloud these picture books to help them learn how to speak in front of a group of people. Have them practice speaking clearly and loudly so that they can easily be heard by an audience.

4. When teaching a grammar or writing lesson, have students use the text of these picture books to identify parts of speech, sentence structure, or writing styles.

5. Have students create a Venn diagram to compare one of the picture books to *V Is for Victory*. Ask students what they think the pros and cons of using a picture book format might be.

6. Have students work together as a class to create their own picture books that tell the stories in these picture books. Have them use the form on page 10 to assign individual responsibilities to class members. In addition, after students have read *Number the Stars* or *Sadako and the Thousand Paper Cranes*, have them make picture books that tells these stories. Have them use the form on page 10 for these assignments as well.

7. After reading these picture books have students describe other picture books they have enjoyed. Ask students if they have read any other picture books about World War II.

8. Divide the class into cooperative learning groups. Give students the opportunity to write and illustrate their own picture books about a topic related to the home front during World War II. Provide the groups with a copy of the form on page 10. Have students use this form to assign individual responsibilities to group members.

Publishing Books in the Classroom

There are many ways to have students publish books in the classroom. The Publishing Center in the classroom should have an adequate supply of materials such as paper, poster board, scissors, markers, and glue. Book covers may be laminated for durability. Have students bind the books by stapling or sewing them with yarn. Allow other students to check out these books by adding library cards and pockets. Students may wish to share the picture books they have made by reading them aloud to younger students. Be sure to place them in the Clouds of War Learning Center and share them at "The Spirit of America" Day

Picture Perfect Publishing Company

STAFF

Authors write rough drafts of text and make suggested revisions by the editors.

Editors revise rough drafts and edit final copies of text.

Binders and publishers organize the revised text and illustrations, bind the book with the cover, and distribute or sell the book.

Authors

_____   _____

Illustrators

_____   _____

Editors

_____   _____

Book Cover Design & Layout

_____   _____

Binding and Publishing

_____   _____

_____   _____

Illustrators create pictures to enhance the text.

Designers determine the layout of the book, design the cover, and make the title and copyright pages.

"Remember Pearl Harbor"

The following questions may be used for research topics, discussion, or critical-thinking activities.

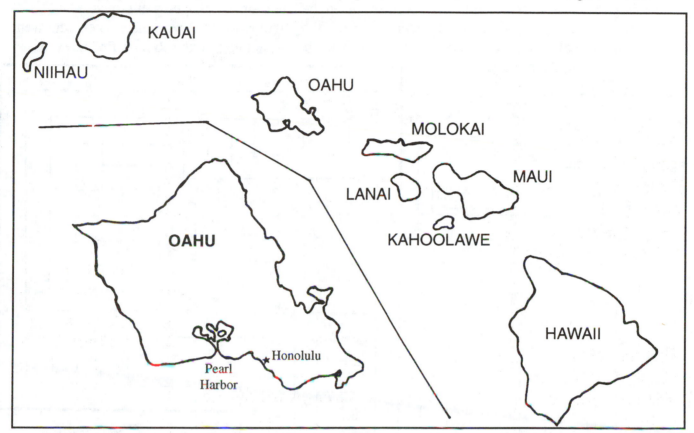

1. Study the map shown above. On which island is Pearl Harbor located? Which major city lies just east of Pearl Harbor?

2. Why did the Japanese choose Pearl Harbor as the first target in their attack against the United States?

3. Who was in command of the American Pacific Fleet when Pearl Harbor was attacked?

4. How many casualties did the United States have at Pearl Harbor in terms of people, ships, and planes?

5. Where is the U.S.S. Arizona Memorial? What does it commemorate?

6. Why did President Franklin D. Roosevelt refer to the bombing of Pearl Harbor as "a date that will live in infamy"?

7. Japanese Admiral Yamamoto feared that the attack on Pearl Harbor would eventually be detrimental to Japan's cause. On what do you think the admiral based this concern?

8. The bombing of Pearl Harbor caused many Americans to treat all Japanese Americans with fear and suspicion. Do you think these feelings were justified? Would you have supported sending Japanese Americans to relocation camps? Why or why not?

Rosie the Riveter

After many men left for war, President Franklin D. Roosevelt called for increased production of wartime goods. As a result, millions of women joined the labor force. Women went to work in shipyards and factories. "Rosie the Riveter" became the symbol associated with the women who went from being housewives to factory workers. In the maze below, help Rosie the Riveter find the way from her home to the factory.

Questions for Discussion

1. After the war, many women who had factory jobs were laid off or replaced by returning veterans. What obstacles do you think were faced by the women who wanted to continue working outside the home?

2. Why do you think American women became united in their desire to be more independent and have the same rights as men after working in factories during World War II?

The Ultimate Sacrifice

World War II has caused more destruction and loss of life than any other war in history. About 70 million people served in either the Allied or Axis armed forces with nearly 17 million of these losing their lives. There is no accurate record of how many civilians lost their lives because bombing raids destroyed many of the records that were needed to account for these deaths.

The table below lists the World War II military deaths for the Allied and the Axis countries. A table is a reference tool that uses columns or rows to organize numerical data. It lists specific numbers, so it may be difficult to visualize the information or make quick comparisons of the data.

Bar graphs are often used to provide a visual representation of the data given in a table. These graphs have rectangular bars that allow for quick and easy comparisons. Using the information in the table below, fill in the bar graph on page 14. Use a different color for each bar to make comparisons even easier.

Allied Countries	Dead
Australia	23,000
Belgium	8,000
Canada	38,000
China	2,200,000
France	211,000
Great Britain	329,000
Poland	320,000
Soviet Union	7,500,000
United States	405,000
Axis Countries	**Dead**
Austria	380,000
Bulgaria	10,000
Finland	82,000
Germany	3,500,000
Hungary	140,000
Italy	77,000
Japan	1,219,000
Romania	300,000

Extending the Activity

1. Which group of countries (Allied or Axis) had the greater number of military deaths?

2. Which Axis country had the greatest number of military deaths? Which Allied country?

3. How many Axis countries had fewer than 100,000 deaths? How many Allied countries?

4. About how many more military deaths did the United States record than Great Britain?

5. About how many fewer military deaths did Japan have than Germany?

The Ultimate Sacrifice *(cont.)*

Make Your Own Bar Graph

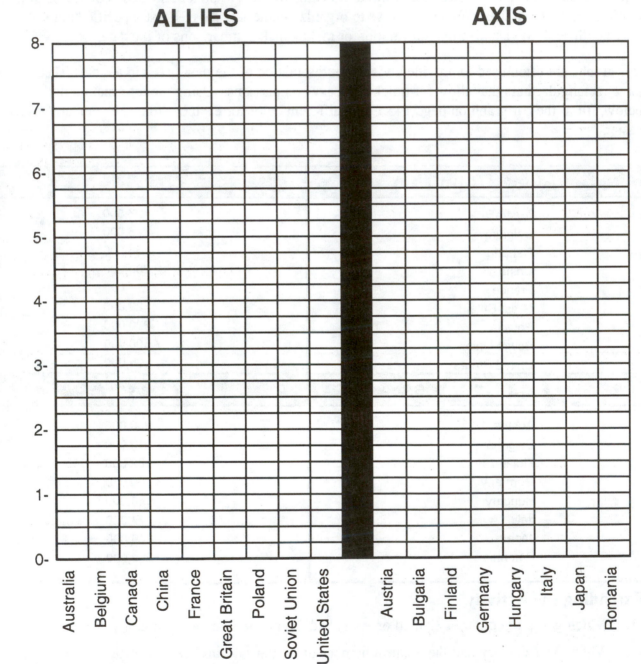

ALLIES　　**AXIS**

Each line represents 250,000 Casualties

8-
7-
6-
5-
4-
3-
2-
1-
0-

Australia, Belgium, Canada, China, France, Great Britain, Poland, Soviet Union, United States, Austria, Bulgaria, Finland, Germany, Hungary, Italy, Japan, Romania

The War Is Over

Understanding cause-and-effect relationships is an important comprehension and critical-thinking skill. This activity may be used as the basis for a discussion at the conclusion of a World War II unit or as a group or individual assignment to evaluate students.

Directions: Fill in the chart to describe a cause-and-effect relationship.

CAUSE *(Why Something Happened)*	EFFECT *(What Happened)*
1. The United States dropped atomic bombs on the cities of Hiroshima and Nagasaki.	1.
2.	2. In 1944, Congress passed the Serviceman's Readjustment Act which was known as the G.I. Bill.
3. The United States government canceled the contracts with defense plants as soon as the war ended.	3.
4.	4. After the war, many factories refused to hire or continue employing women and minority workers.
5. Nuclear weapons were developed.	5.
6.	6. There was a housing shortage in the United States following World War II.
7. Many women were not content to give up their factory jobs and return to traditional female roles.	7.
8.	8. The Marshall Plan was established.
9. The Soviet Union wanted Germany to be a Communist country, and the Allies wanted to establish a democratic government.	9.

Extending Cause-and-Effect

The demands in research and development during the war years (1941-1945) resulted in scientists making many discoveries and inventions. List some of the American discoveries or inventions that were developed during World War II. See if you can explain why the war "caused" those discoveries or inventions.

World War II

Directions: Use *V Is for Victory* and other reference books to determine the answers to the clues. Then fill in the puzzle.

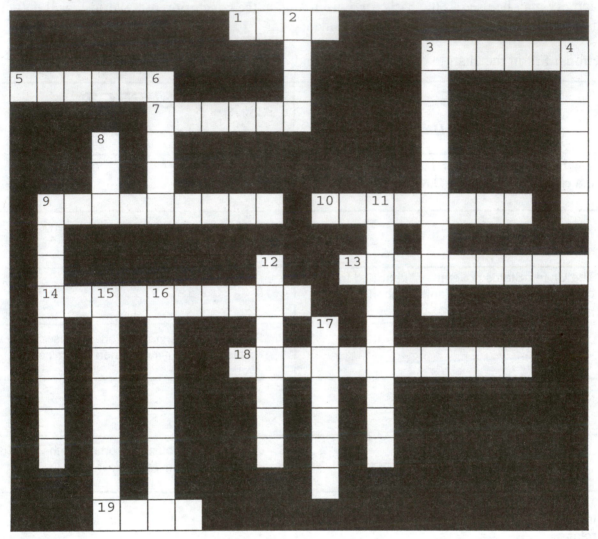

Across

1. Military leader in control of Japan during the war
3. Dictator of Germany during the war
5. Ruthless leader of the Soviet Union during the war
7. Countries fighting against the Axis powers
9. City in Japan on which the first atomic bomb was dropped
10. A person who has complete power and authority over a country
13. Dictator of Italy during the war
14. Supreme commander of the Allied Forces during the war
18. American base in Hawaii that was bombed by Japan
19. The alliance of Germany, Italy, and Japan

Down

2. People persecuted by the Nazis because of their religion
3. The mass murder of European Jews
4. To allow each person only certain amounts of foods, gasoline, and other goods
6. German political party in power during the war
8. Initials of the 32nd president of the United States
9. Term given to the United States mainland during the war
11. Prime minister of Great Britain during the war
12. A soldier who returns home from war
15. Emblem on the Nazi flag
16. Japanese city on which the second atomic bomb was dropped
17. Became the 33rd president of the United States

Number the Stars

by Lois Lowry

Summary

This 1990 Newbery Award book vividly depicts the intense drama experienced by the Jewish people living in Denmark during World War II. The story centers around two close-knit families, the Rosens and the Johansens. The Rosen family is Jewish and in great danger of being "relocated" by the Nazis. Annemarie Johansen is only ten years old, but she must help smuggle her best friend, Ellen Rosen, out of Denmark and into Sweden where Jewish people could find refuge.

Ellen poses as Annemarie's sister as they journey to the coast. There, Ellen is reunited with her parents. Then, the Johansen family hides the small group of Jewish refugees in a secret compartment on a fishing boat that takes them to neutral Sweden. Every step of this dangerous mission is filled with suspense and intrigue.

This historical fiction story wonderfully describes the courage and commitment of the Danish Resistance forces as they miraculously smuggled nearly the entire Jewish population of 7,000 across the sea to Sweden. The title of the book, Number the Stars, is taken from the biblical psalm that accurately conveys the spirit and faith of the Danish people during the most trying period of time in their history. "It is He who heals the broken in spirit and binds up their wounds, He who numbers the stars one by one...."

Sample Plan

Lesson 1

- Introduce Denmark and its role in World War II (page 18).
- Read Chapters 1 and 2 in *Number the Stars*.
- Construct WW II Diaries (pages 40-41) and write about the topic for Lesson 1 (page 42).
- Complete critical-thinking questions and activities for Lesson 1 (page 20).
- Compare Denmark's form of government to that of the United States.

Lesson 2

- Read Chapters 3 and 4.
- Complete critical-thinking questions and activities for Lesson 2 (page 20).
- Write about the diary topic for Lesson 2 (page 42).
- Discuss the issues and events surrounding the Holocaust (pages 22-23).

- Relate aspects of the Holocaust to current world events. Summarize these events on the World News Update form (page 24).
- Construct a World News Update bulletin board for students to display newspaper articles related to current events (pages 23-24).

Lesson 3

- Read Chapters 5 and 6.
- Complete critical-thinking questions and activities for Lesson 3 (page 20).
- Write about the diary topic for Lesson 3 (page 42).
- Discuss the importance of secret codes. Invite students to devise their own codes and exchange messages about WW II.
- Discuss how current media coverage of a war might affect the military's ability to keep critical strategies a secret.

Sample Plan *(cont.)*

Sample Plan (cont.)

Lesson 4

- Read Chapters 7 and 8.
- Complete critical-thinking questions and activities for Lesson 4 (page 20).
- Write about the diary topic for Lesson 4 (page 42).
- Analyze the friendship between Annemarie and Ellen.

Lesson 5

- Read Chapters 9 and 10.
- Complete critical-thinking questions and activities for Lesson 5 (page 20).
- Write about the diary topic for Lesson 5 (page 42).
- Discuss adult's dishonesty in order to protect children.

Lesson 6

- Read Chapters 11 and 12.
- Complete critical-thinking questions and activities for Lesson 6 (page 20).
- Write about the diary topic for Lesson 6 (page 42).
- Do research to learn more about the rescue of Danish Jews (pages 25-26).
- Discuss the qualities of the Danish Resistance Fighters.

- Do the Wordsearch for *A Bright Star Over Denmark* (page 27).
- Continue adding to the World News Update bulletin board (pages 23-24).

Lesson 7

- Read Chapters 13, 14, and 15.
- Complete critical-thinking questions and activities for Lesson 7 (page 21).
- Write about the diary topic for Lesson 7 (page 42).
- Discuss the character traits of Annemarie. After reading *Sadako and the Thousand Paper Cranes,* compare Annemarie to Sadako (page 48).

Lesson 8

- Read Chapters 16, 17, and Afterward.
- Complete critical-thinking questions and activities for Lesson 8 (page 21).
- Write about the diary topic for Lesson 8 (page 42).
- Complete an analysis of the main characters described in *Number the Stars* (page 21).
- Discuss *Number the Stars* as a work of historical fiction (page 47).

Overview of Activities

SETTING THE STAGE

1. Have students locate Denmark on a world map. Have them compare European borders of today with those during WW II (pages 59-60).
2. Have students do research to learn about the role of the Danish Resistance during WW II.
3. Review WW II Vocabulary (page 43).
4. Demonstrate how to construct WW II Diaries for daily writing activities (page 40-41).
5. Send home the parent letter to inform them about this unit (page 76).
6. Set up Clouds of War Learning Center and appropriate bulletin boards (pages 72-74).

Overview of Activities *(cont.)*

ENJOYING THE BOOK

1. Continue with Headline News activities (pages 44-45). Have students decide which World War II events from *Number the Stars* would make front page news stories and assign these as individual or class writing activities.

2. Have students examine maps to analyze the changes in Germany's borders during the twentieth century (pages 59-60).

3. Students should continue working on their own picture books from the Picture Perfect Publishing Company (pages 8-10). This project should be used throughout the unit as students gather information and complete the writing and publishing process. These picture books may be published by individual students or by cooperative learning groups. After the books are completed, they should be placed in the Clouds of War Learning Center (page 72).

4. Have students do research to discover which other groups worked to save Jewish people during WW II. Nonfiction books, such as *Rescue —The Story of How Gentiles Saved Jews During the Holocaust* by Milton Meltzer and *The Holocaust - The Fire that Raged* by Seymour Rossel (bibliography, page 78), may be used as resources.

EXTENDING THE BOOK

1. Encourage students to read other works of literature about the Holocaust, such as *The Devil's Arithmetic* by Jane Yolen (bibliography, page 78).

2. Continue adding to the World News Update by displaying summaries that students have written using newspaper articles about oppression and persecution in current world events (pages 23-24).

3. Model how to write a Super Simple Summary (pages 28-29) using another recently published book about WW II entitled *Stepping on the Cracks* by Mary D. Hahn. Then have students use the Super Simple Summary form (page 29) to write a summary of *Number the Stars*.

   If students are not ready to write a summary of the entire book, they may use this same form to write a summary of each chapter. Students gain experience by writing short summaries of what they read each day. The same format should be used for summarizing an entire book or a chapter, since the same elements will still be addressed.

   When summarizing, students should ask themselves the following questions: Who? When? Where? What? How? Why?

   Use the Super Simple Summary form to assess students' understanding of the story and to identify which students are still having difficulty writing summaries. Once they have mastered the skill of summarizing, students can use the Super Simple Summary form to summarize any book.

4. Continue with Big Book activities for The Long Road to Peace (pages 70-71). Be sure materials needed to complete this project are available in the Clouds of War Learning Center (page 72).

5. Continue planning "The Spirit of America" Day activities (pages 68-69).

Critical-Thinking Questions and Activities

Lesson 1

1. Predict what might happen if Annemarie, Ellen, and Kirsti are seen again by the same two Nazi soldiers on the street of Osterbrogade.

2. Why did the Danish people still hold King Christian X in such high regard even though he did not put up a fight when the Nazis invaded their country?

Lesson 2

3. Analyze the significance of Mrs. Hirsch's shop being closed.

4. How accurate was Annemarie's statement "...now I think that all of Denmark must be bodyguard for the Jews"? Do you think she realized the significance of her statement at this point in the story?

5. Write a description of the plan the Johansens had if the Nazi soldiers came to their apartment looking for Ellen and her family.

Lesson 3

6. Why did Annemarie rip the necklace from Ellen's neck?

7. Why did the Nazi soldier suspect that Ellen was not a Johansen? What changed his mind?

Lesson 4

8. During wartime, many messages had to be sent using secret codes. Deduce the meaning of the telephone conversation between Papa and Uncle Henrik in Chapter 7.

9. Why was it important for the girls not to talk to anyone while staying at Uncle Henrik's house?

10. Give two reasons why Annemarie was so certain that Great-aunt Birte did not exist. What can you conclude is the reason for the story about Great-aunt Birte's death?

Lesson 5

11. Paraphrase what Uncle Henrik was trying to explain to Annemarie when he said, "..it is much easier to be brave if you do not know everything."

12. How did Mama's quick thinking prevent the Nazis from opening the casket? What do you think is in the casket?

Lesson 6

13. Annemarie came to the realization that the Rosens and the rest of this small group of Jewish people had not lost their sense of pride. Examine the sources of pride in the Jewish people and the Danish Resistance Fighters and compare these with the things you consider sources of pride in your own life.

14. Make a list of the things that could possibly have gone wrong when Mama was leading the Rosens to Uncle Henrik's boat.

Critical-Thinking Questions and Activities *(cont.)*

Lesson 7

15. Predict what you think is in the packet Annemarie must take to Uncle Henrik before he sails for Sweden.

16. How do you think Mama felt about sending Annemarie with the packet to Uncle Henrik?

17. Compare and contrast Annemarie's trip through the woods with that of the fairy tale character Little Red Riding Hood.

18. Give examples of how Annemarie played the role of a silly little girl instead of the ten-year-old girl who had really become wise beyond her years.

Lesson 8

19. Predict whether you think Annemarie and Ellen will ever see each other again. Explain your prediction.

20. What was in the packet that Annemarie brought to Uncle Henrik? Why was this packet truly a matter of life or death for Uncle Henrik's precious human cargo?

21. What had Annemarie learned about the deaths of Peter and her older sister Lise?

22. The title of this book, *Number the Stars,* comes from the biblical psalm Peter read while the frightened group of Jews huddled in Uncle Henrik's living room. Write a new title for this book that would help the reader know what this book is about.

23. On the last page of the afterward in the book, there is the actual letter of a Danish Resistance Fighter which he wrote the night before he was executed by the Nazis. From reading his last words, what can you tell about the kind of person this young man was?

Character Analysis

Analyze the qualities and character traits of the main characters named below.

Annemarie   **Ellen**   **Uncle Henrik**   **Peter**   **Annemarie's Mother**

Ask yourself the following questions:

- How would you describe the qualities and traits of these characters?
- How do you know what kind of person each character is?
- How are these characters similar?
- How are these characters different?
- Is there a common trait that you feel many of these characters share?
- How does the author depict the qualities of the Nazi soldiers in contrast to these characters?
- Are there any similarities between the Nazi soldiers and any of these characters?
- Are there any qualities or traits exhibited by these characters that might prove to be weaknesses for someone trying to smuggle Jews to safety?

The Holocaust

The Holocaust is defined as the mass murder of European Jews during World War II by Adolf Hitler's Nazi soldiers. A brief synopsis of the events leading up to and including the Holocaust begins below and concludes on page 23. This summary may be used as a teaching aid or as a guide for discussion. Several classroom activities that address the events of the Holocaust follow this summary. It is important to be as forthright as possible with students when discussing this complex issue. Explain that it is important to study and analyze the dark, somber periods in history so that tragedies such as the Holocaust will never happen again.

Adolf Hitler's Plan to Conquer the World

At the end of World War I, the Allies forced the Central Powers to sign the Treaty of Versailles. This treaty said that Germany was guilty of starting the war and therefore must be punished. The treaty took away one-tenth of the German land. It restricted Germans from building up their military or manufacturing large weapons. The treaty also forced them to pay the Allies large sums of money to reimburse those countries for expenses incurred during the war. It left Germany a poor country with many Germans feeling betrayed by their new democratic government for signing the treaty. Adolf Hitler, who was the head of the Nazi Party (National Socialist German Worker's Party), easily took control over the weak government.

Hitler told the German people that Germany's problems were caused by the Treaty of Versailles and by the Jewish people. The Jews became an easy scapegoat since many people believed that they were to blame for the death of Jesus. Therefore, Hitler decided the solution to Germany's problems was to get more land and to get rid of the Jews. Because so many Germans felt desperate, Hitler soon had a large following.

As Hitler's power and support grew, he began building an army and preparing for war. Eventually, Hitler joined forces with the Italian dictator, Benito Mussolini. Mussolini was also dissatisfied with the terms of the Treaty of Versailles. Japan later joined Germany and Italy to form the Axis powers. Together they began attacking other countries.

As the Nazis forcibly took control of many European countries, Hitler began to pursue the second phase of his plan—the extermination of the Jews. Not only did Hitler plan to completely wipe out the entire Jewish population, but he also targeted other groups such as Gypsies, Poles, Slavs, physically or mentally disabled persons, and anyone who opposed him.

The Nazis built special prisons called concentration camps throughout Europe. Jews were forced to leave their jobs, and Jewish-owned businesses were vandalized. Millions of Jews were eventually sent to concentration or death camps such as Auschwitz, Treblinka, Belzec, and Majdanek. These camps included gas chambers where thousands of Jews were killed with poison gas and their bodies burned in huge furnaces. Some of the camps had factories where the prisoners were literally worked to death. Many of the Jews died from disease, starvation, or torture. Doctors sometimes performed cruel medical experiments on the prisoners. Anyone found to be too sick or old to work was killed in the gas chamber.

The Holocaust *(cont.)*

By the time World War II ended, about 6 million out of an estimated 8.3 million Jews living in German-occupied Europe were killed. Denmark is the only country where Resistance Forces were able to smuggle most of their Jewish population into neutral Sweden to escape the Nazi soldiers.

Most people around the world were unaware of the atrocities that were taking place in the concentration camps. When the war ended, the Allied troops saw first-hand the gruesome sights at these camps. It was then that the rest of the world was forced to face the reality of the Holocaust.

Classroom Activities

An effective method of addressing the subject of the Holocaust is to connect it to a current events or a social studies lesson. Using the worksheet on page 24, have students locate and summarize current newspaper articles that describe people from around the world who are suffering from oppression or persecution such as civil war, economic unrest, or racism. Allow students to share their summaries and then display them on a bulletin board similar to the one suggested below.

WORLD NEWS UPDATE

"Those who cannot remember the past are condemned to repeat it."
—*George Santayana*, **Life of Reason**

WORLD NEWS UPDATE

TODAY'S NEWS IS TOMORROW'S HISTORY

A Bright Star Over Denmark

The Miracle Rescue of the Danish Jews

On April 9, 1940, Germany invaded the Scandinavian country of Denmark. King Christian X, the ruler of Denmark, knew his small country was no match for Hitler's forces. He surrendered after only a few hours of fighting. The Nazis decided to keep the Danish government in power as long as its officials met their demands. During the next three years of the German occupation, Danish Resistance Forces were formed and began to sabotage factories and transportation systems. As a result, the Nazis took over the government in August 1943.

In October 1943, Jewish people living in Denmark learned that the Nazis were planning to round up the entire Jewish population and send them to death camps. Within hours, over 7,000 Danish Jews were safely hidden in the homes of non-Jewish neighbors and friends. On the night of the Nazis' roundup, 284 Jews were arrested. The Nazis continued to search over the next month, and 200 more Danish Jews were located and sent to death camps.

Small groups of Jews, totaling approximately 7,200 people, were smuggled by Danish Resistance Fighters to fishing villages along the coast. From there, they were hidden in fishing boats in order to cross the 15-mile (9.3-kilometer) channel to Sweden, a neutral country. Many Resistance Fighters lost their lives taking part in this smuggling operation.

The Jews who were arrested by the Nazis were not forgotten. The Danish government persisted in knowing their whereabouts and even inspected the camps where they were being held. Nazi records indicate that 51 Danish Jews died in these camps from natural causes. The Danish authorities believe these deaths were the result of atrocious living conditions in the camps. There is no record of any Danish Jew being killed in a gas chamber by the Nazis.

After World War II when the Jews returned to their homes in Denmark, they found that their fellow countrymen had cared for and protected their property. Their homes were the same as when they had left to escape the Nazis.

The Danish people were certainly courageous and heroic. Their story provided a bright ray of hope during the dark days of World War II.

Following A Bright Star Over Denmark

1. The map below shows the European boundaries following World War I. Use the map to locate and color Denmark, Sweden, and Germany. Examine where Denmark is in relationship to Germany and Sweden. Locate Copenhagen, the capital of Denmark, which is the main setting in *Number the Stars*. How did Denmark's geographical location and features play a major role in the success of smuggling Danish Jews to Sweden?

2. Research to discover why Sweden remained neutral during World War II even though its neighboring countries had fallen victim to the Nazi war machine.

3. The Danish Resistance movement was primarily organized by very young men and women. If you had been a teenager living in Denmark in 1943, would you have been one of the Resistance Fighters? What qualities would you need in order to participate in this colossal operation at such a high risk?

4. How do you think the successful rescue of Danish Jews helped to spark Resistance efforts in other parts of German-occupied Europe?

5. Identify any current events or situations in the world today in which one group of people may be the target of oppression or injustice by its government. Are there any groups, similar to the Danish Resistance Fighters, who are striving to fight these injustices? Are these groups trying to fight this oppression using peaceful or violent tactics?

European Boundaries Following World War I

Wordsearch for
A Bright Star Over Denmark

Can you find the following words dealing with the heroic rescue of the Danish Jews? The words are placed backwards, forward, diagonally, up, and down.

Sweden	Villages	Resistance	Rescue
Holocaust	Germany	Death Camps	Round Up
Sabotage	Jews	Channel	King Christian X
Smuggle	Fishing Boats	Neutral	Nazis
Coast	Courage	Denmark	Hitler

```
G S B S V H R H F P L D C F J B V V G C M R F S
E S Y H A N N B L B C K Q B M L C N Y J E R Y K
R G F H C B F F X N H L C V Z J Q N G S B T R S
C O A S T A O B G N I H S I F N A Z I S E A S R
N Q W R W R C T B H A M O T G M M S G U M P V D
L E L V U E R S A N U I H L R P T N C N M R G K
J P S P I O D V N G Z V T E O A M S E A L C P F
G H B Z W L C E G R E B G S N C E D C U Y J W V
R D I B B L L L N P O J J C I R A H K Z T B R W
T B B T K W E I S N G U E S B R T U F K T R B P
D X P V L X K R A W Z V N Y D A H V S G Q F A R
F J K W G E S R X G G Z Y D E L T C R T X R L L
V S D T Y S R N N K E J V D U S Y B G X H G Y Q
C M W G M G Y B H P T S G Z V P S N H N S X T M
Z S H F G W K J T G N V T W S Y B F Q L I F Z C
J S W F L C T B W F W R W T M F H V P Z Y K H J
P C W T K S C Q Z H P Z W G W D G X N S P B Q M
```

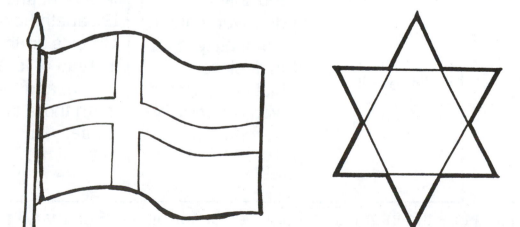

What was the significance of the Star of David in the story *Number the Stars*?

Super Simple Summary

An excellent way to evaluate reading comprehension and written language is to have students write summaries. Many students have a great deal of difficulty distinguishing between main ideas and details. Therefore, it is important to provide them with a model for how to write summaries.

Begin by reading aloud *Stepping on the Cracks* by Mary D. Hahn (bibliography, page 78). Use a transparency of the following plan to show students how to organize a summary for this book. If you prefer to use a different story, make a transparency of the form on page 29 for your model.

SUPER SIMPLE SUMMARY

Stepping on the Cracks
(TITLE)

Mary Downing Hahn
(AUTHOR)

WHO?	WHEN/WHERE?	WHAT?	HOW/WHY?
Who are the main characters?	When/Where does the story take place?	What are the goals of the main characters or what problems must they solve?	How do the characters reach their goals or solve their problems? If so, how? If not, why not?
Margaret and Elizabeth—sixth graders who are best friends	1944-1945 (World War II)	Margaret and Elizabeth discover that the worst bully in their class is hiding his brother who is a military deserter.	Margaret and Elizabeth help Gordy's brother instead of turning him in, and they learn there are no easy answers in wartime.
Gordy Smith— classmate who is a bully	College Hill— small town		

Now help students use the information from the "Super Simple Summary" plan to write a rough draft of a summary.

SUPER SIMPLE SUMMARY

_____
(Title)

_____
(Author)

WHO?	WHEN/WHERE?	WHAT?	HOW/WHY?
Who are the main characters?	When/Where does the story take place?	What are the goals of the main characters, or what problems must they solve?	How do the characters reach their goals or solve their problems?

Sadako and the Thousand Paper Cranes

by Eleanor Coerr

Summary

One of the bitter realities of any war is that there are always innocent victims on both sides. Sadako and the Thousand Paper Cranes tenderly and poignantly depicts this tragedy of war by describing the life of a Japanese girl and her family. Sadako Sasaki was two years old when the United States Air Force dropped an atom bomb on the city of Hiroshima. Ten years later, Sadako died of leukemia resulting from the bomb's radiation.

Sadako and the Thousand Paper Cranes *is based on the true story of Sadako Sasaki who lived in Japan from 1943 until 1955. While in the hospital, one of her friends brought her a folded paper crane as a good luck charm. According to an old Japanese tale, the crane was supposed to live for a thousand years. If a sick person folded one thousand paper cranes, the gods would restore that person's health. Sadako began her task of folding the paper cranes. She thought that this would surely take away the dreaded disease and restore the smiles to the faces of her family and friends. There were 644 cranes hanging from the ceiling of Sadako's hospital room when she died on October 25, 1955, at the age of twelve. Her classmates finished the task and folded three-hundred fifty-six cranes so that all one-thousand could be buried with Sadako.*

This tale of hope, courage, and heroism soon spread throughout Japan. At Peace Park in Hiroshima, a statue of Sadako holding a golden crane was erected as a lasting tribute to all the children killed by the atom bomb and its aftereffects. Sadako's story gives a candid and realistic view of how the atom bomb caused casualties in Japan long after the war was over.

Sample Plan

Lesson 1

- Begin exploring information about Japan and its culture (page 31).
- Introduce the effects of World War II from the Japanese perspective (page 31).
- Read the Prologue and Chapters 1 and 2 in *Sadako and the Thousand Paper Cranes*.
- Complete critical-thinking questions and activities for Lesson 1 (page 34).
- Construct WW II Diaries (pages 40-41) and write about the topic for Lesson 1 (page 42).
- Compete in a relay race when researching facts about Memorial Day celebrations (page 36).

Lesson 2

- Read Chapters 3 and 4.
- Complete critical-thinking questions and activities for Lesson 2 (page 34).
- Write about the diary topic for Lesson 2 (page 42).
- Learn more about the development of the atomic bomb (pages 52-53).
- Do the Atom Bomb Wordsearch (page 54).

Sample Plan (cont.)

Sample Plan (cont.)

Lesson 3

- Read Chapters 5 and 6.
- Complete critical-thinking questions and activities for Lesson 3 (page 34).
- Write about the diary topic for Lesson 3 (page 42).
- Join the Folded Crane Club and learn more about the Japanese art form of origami (page 37).

Lesson 4

- Read Chapters 7, 8, and 9.
- Complete critical-thinking questions and activities for Lesson 4 (page 35).
- Write about the diary topic for Lesson 4 (page 42).
- Discuss the character traits of Sadako. Compare the traits and qualities of Sadako to those of Annemarie in *Number the Stars* (page 48).

Lesson 5

- Read and discuss the Epilogue.
- Construct a time line using events from the story (page 35).
- Write about the diary topic for Lesson 5 (page 42).
- Identify the elements of a biography. Complete a biographical data sheet about Sadako. Use the information from the data sheet to write a short biography (page 38).
- Analyze the significance of Sadako's life. Predict what Sadako might have accomplished if she had lived. Then, make personal predictions about the future (page 39).
- Make a pamphlet that tells about *Sadako and the Thousand Paper Cranes* (page 75).
- Locate and read newspaper or magazine articles that tell about current events in Japan.

Overview of Activities
SETTING THE STAGE

1. On a world map, show where Japan is located. Then point out where it is in relationship to the United States and Pearl Harbor (Oahu, Hawaii). Have students find the cities of Hiroshima and Nagasaki in Japan.

2. Review the WW II Vocabulary that is pertinent to this story (page 43).

3. Assemble the Clouds of War Learning Center (page 72). Then, display the Japan Bulletin Board for students' haiku and origami (page 74).

4. If you have not already done so, send home the parent letter informing them that your class is studying WW II (page 76). This letter also invites parents to help gather materials for the Clouds of War Learning Center.

5. When planning "The Spirit of America" Day, plan how to honor the Japanese as well as other cultures living in America (page 68).

6. Explore the Japanese language by doing the Context Clue Connections (page 33).

Overview of Activities *(cont.)*

ENJOYING THE BOOK

1. Have students join The Folded Crane Club and make origami cranes (page 37).

2. Analyze the components of a front-page news story and decide which WW II events associated with *Sadako and the Thousand Paper Cranes* would be written as headline news stories. Have students make a newspaper with stories that they write (pages 44-45).

3. Continue studying the Japanese culture by having students write a type of poetry called haiku (page 46).

4. Explore President Truman's difficult decision to drop the atomic bomb (page 55).

5. Imagine what Sadako wrote in her letters to her classmates. Have each student write a letter. Then bind all of the letters to make your own class book called *Kokeshi.*

6. Have students pretend they have been chosen to speak at the dedication ceremonies for Sadako's monument at Peace Park in Hiroshima. Have them write their speeches and present them to the class.

7. Ask students if they have ever known someone who was critically ill. Have them describe their experiences.

EXTENDING THE BOOK

1. Analyze the characteristics of historical fiction by comparing *Sadako and the Thousand Paper Cranes* and *Number the Stars* (page 47). Invite students to read other historical fiction books. Then, have them write their own historical fiction story. Ask volunteers to share their stories with the class.

2. Continue exploring Japanese culture with Origami on Parade (page 62). Have students discover how to make other patterns using library books about origami.

3. Continue working on Big Book—The Long Road To Peace to extend their knowledge about Japan's role in WW II and other wars involving Japan (pages 70-71).

4. Explore the effects of WW II on the Japanese living in the U.S. at the time of the bombing of Pearl Harbor: The Sad Mistake (page 65).

5. Invite a person of Japanese descent or someone who has recently visited Japan to be a guest speaker in your classroom. The guest speaker may wish to show students actual items from Japan.

6. Have students write a persuasive letter to President Truman asking him to drop or not to drop the atomic bomb on Japan (page 55).

7. Invite someone who speaks Japanese to give a language lesson to your class after students have used Context Clue Connections (page 33).

8. Have students use reference books to find out about the benefits of atomic research. Have students make a chart that shows the benefits and problems of atomic research.

9. Continue planning "The Spirit of America" Day (page 69).

Context Clue Connections

One way to learn more about people whose culture is different from your own is to study their language. Use context clues to translate the italicized Japanese words in the following sentences.

Note: When pronouncing Japanese words, equal emphasis is given to each syllable.

1. Sadako was only a young *kodomo* when the atom bomb was dropped.
   kodomo: _____

2. Sadako was in the bamboo class at the *gakko* she attended.
   gakko: _____

3. Many people have installed answering machines to record messages when they are unable to answer their *denwa*.
   denwa: _____

4. Japanese and American children are taught to be polite and always say *doozo* when they want something and thank you when they receive it.
   doozo: _____

5. The mother tucked in her small child, turned off the lights, and said, *"Oyasumi nasai!"*
   Oyasumi nasai: _____

Now it is your turn to try writing sentences that include Japanese words. Write a paragraph in which you substitute Japanese words and phrases for English ones, using the chart below. Be sure the context helps convey the meaning of the Japanese words and phrases. Exchange your paper with a classmate, and see if you can translate each other's paragraphs.

English	Japanese	English	Japanese
cat	*neko*	no	*iie*
dinner	*yuuhan*	nose	*hana*
dog	*inu*	small	*chiisai*
father	*otoosan*	stove	*hibachi*
fish	*sakana*	tea	*ocha*
good-bye	*sayonara*	teacher	*sensei*
grandfather	*ojiisan*	umbrella	*kasa*
grandmother	*obaasan*	Good morning!	*O-hayoo gozaimasu!*
house	*uchi*	How are you?	*Ikaga desu ka?*
money	*okane*	What is it?	*Nan desuka?*
mother	*okaasan*		

Critical-Thinking Questions and Activities

Lesson 1

1. Based solely on information given in the prologue, give at least two other reasons why Sadako became a heroine in the hearts of the Japanese people.

2. Summarize the significance of August sixth in the lives of the Japanese people.

3. Even though it had been nine years since the atom bomb was dropped on the city of Hiroshima, why were people still dying from its effects?

4. Throughout this story, you will notice that the Japanese emphasize good fortune and good luck signs. List two good luck signs mentioned by Sadako in the first two chapters. Then, list as many good luck signs as you can from the American culture, such as a rabbit's foot. What can you conclude might be similar and different about the beliefs in omens of good fortune for these two cultures?

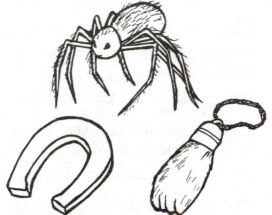

5. Sadako says that she can remember the "Thunderbolt" even though she was barely two years old. Describe the earliest childhood memory you can recall and tell how old you were.

Lesson 2

6. What goal has Sadako set for herself? Predict how Sadako's "secret" will affect whether or not she attains her goal.

7. Select a time in your life when you successfully reached a goal. Compare and contrast your feelings to those of Sadako after her team won the relay race.

8. Explain why Sadako put her hands over her ears when someone mentioned leukemia.

9. What details in the story support the idea that Sadako knew much more about what was happening to her than she let on?

Lesson 3

10. Summarize the story of the golden crane.

11. What qualities has Sadako's friend, Chizuko, demonstrated?

12. Compare and contrast Sadako's beliefs about good luck charms with those of her friend, Chizuko.

13. "...Sadako folded more cranes to keep up her courage." Pretend that you are Sadako's classmate and friend and that you have gone to visit her in the hospital. What words of encouragement would you give to Sadako?

14. Identify some of the symptoms of leukemia that Sadako began to experience.

15. Compare and contrast Sadako with her new friend, Kenji. Include both biographical facts as well as character traits and qualities.

Critical-Thinking Questions
and Activities *(cont.)*

Lesson 4

16. What was Kokeshi?

17. What was Eiji's special present for Sadako?

18. Describe the Japanese holiday of O Bon.

19. Explain these lines from the story: "A bigger pain was growing deep inside of her. It was the fear of dying."

20. Doctors always talk about a patient's will to live. How would you describe Sadako's will to live? Could you sense a change in her hope and courage as the story progressed? Give details from the story to support your opinion.

21. Why did Sadako cry when her family gave her the silk kimono?

22. Sadako described her family as a "warm, loving circle where she would always be. Nothing could ever change that." Describe the role each member of Sadako's family (Mr. Sasaki, Mrs. Sasaki, Masahiro, Mitsue, and Eiji) played in her fight to survive.

Lesson 5

Complete the time line shown below using events described in *Sadako and the Thousand Paper Cranes,* along with other historical data. You may also wish to draw additional lines and include other significant events, such as Chizuki gives Sadako her first crane; Sadako's friend, Kenji, dies; Sadako's class folds 356 more cranes; Sadako's class publishes her letters in a book called *Kokeshi;* and young people begin collecting money for a monument to honor Sadako.

Time Line of *Sadako and the Thousand Paper Cranes*

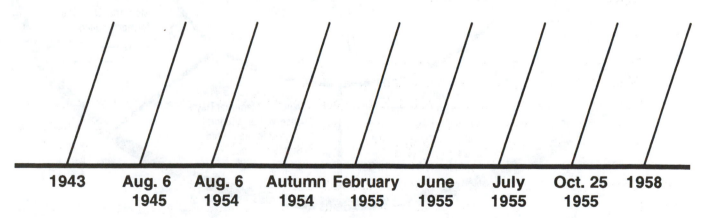

| 1943 | Aug. 6 1945 | Aug. 6 1954 | Autumn 1954 | February 1955 | June 1955 | July 1955 | Oct. 25 1955 | 1958 |

Research Relay

Sadako's mother told her, "You must not call it a carnival. Every year on August sixth we remember those who died when the atom bomb was dropped on our city. It is our memorial day."

Like Japan, the United States has a Memorial Day. How much do you know about this holiday? Use reference books to compete in the relay race shown below. Work as quickly as you can to correctly answer each question about Memorial Day in the United States. Record the time your team begins and completes the relay. Wait for all of the teams to finish. Then check the answers. The team with the best score and the shortest time is the winner.

Memorial Day Relay Race

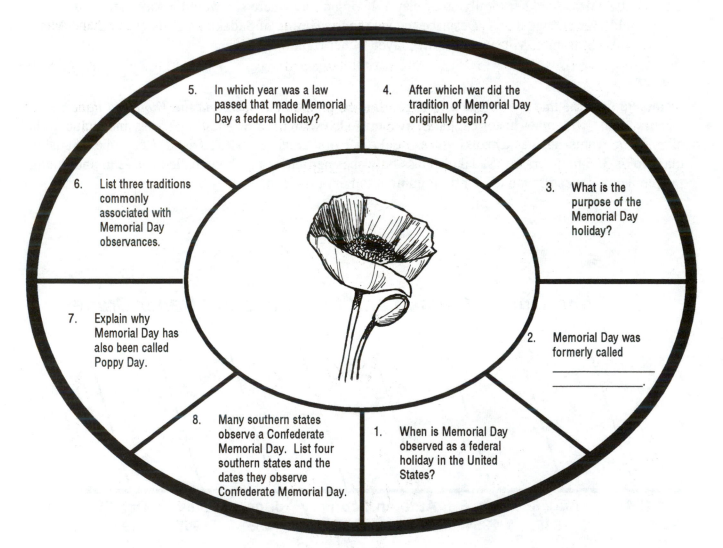

5. In which year was a law passed that made Memorial Day a federal holiday?

4. After which war did the tradition of Memorial Day originally begin?

6. List three traditions commonly associated with Memorial Day observances.

3. What is the purpose of the Memorial Day holiday?

7. Explain why Memorial Day has also been called Poppy Day.

2. Memorial Day was formerly called

_____
_____.

8. Many southern states observe a Confederate Memorial Day. List four southern states and the dates they observe Confederate Memorial Day.

1. When is Memorial Day observed as a federal holiday in the United States?

The Folded Crane Club

The Folded Crane Club was formed in honor of Sadako Sasaki. Follow the steps below to learn how to make an origami crane like the ones Sadako and her friend made.

1. Fold your square four times as shown below.
2. Using a diagonal fold as the center, fold the left and right edges into the center line to make a kite shape.
3. Repeat kite fold on each corner. Your opened paper should be creased as shown.
4. Fold the paper in half to make a triangle. Hold it at the star and fold the right side up to meet the top of the triangle.
5. Release the fold and make the same fold inside out, with the fold coming between the front and back of the large triangle. Repeat on left side. Sharpen the creases.
6. Holding the diamond shape at the star, do the same inside out, fold on the broken lines to form an upside down kite shape. You will make four folds like this: right, left, turnover, right, left. Sharpen the creases.
7. Hold the point with the star and fold down the top flap at the broken line. Turn the shape over and repeat the fold on the other side.
8. Fold down the right flap at the broken line. Release and make the same fold inside out. Repeat on the left side.
9. Turn the shape as shown and fold the end of the point at the broken line to form the crane's head. Release and make the same fold inside out. Fold down the top flap at broken line to make a wing. Turn over and fold the other wing.
10. Roll the wings around a pencil to give a curved shape.

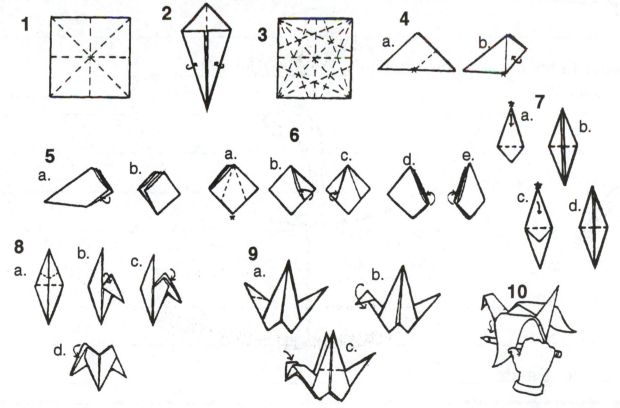

A Biography: The Perfect Tribute

A biography is the factual story of a person's life. When you write a biography, use a variety of descriptive words that will make the story more interesting and help give the reader a mental image of the events in the person's life.

Fill out the biographical data sheet shown below using information from *Sadako and the Thousand Paper Cranes*. Then use the data sheet to write a brief biography of Sadako Sasaki. You may wish to organize the biography in an outline or a story map before you begin writing your rough draft. After you have written your rough draft, revise and edit it before writing your final draft.

Biographical Data Sheet

Name:_____

Family Member(s): _____

Date of Birth: _____

Place of Birth:_____

Education:_____

Significant Events or Other Important Facts about This Person's Life: _____

_____

_____

Special Talents or Achievements: _____

_____

_____

Special Contributions: _____

_____

_____

Date of Death: _____

Place of Death:_____

Reason for Death: _____

38

Prediction Pentagon

Throughout most of the story, Sadako never lost hope that the thousand paper cranes would bring a miracle and that her health would be restored. What might have happened if Sadako had won her battle against leukemia? Use the pentagon below to list five predictions about events or accomplishments in Sadako's life if she had lived. Be sure to explore all avenues of her life, such as education, career, family, and contributions to Japan.

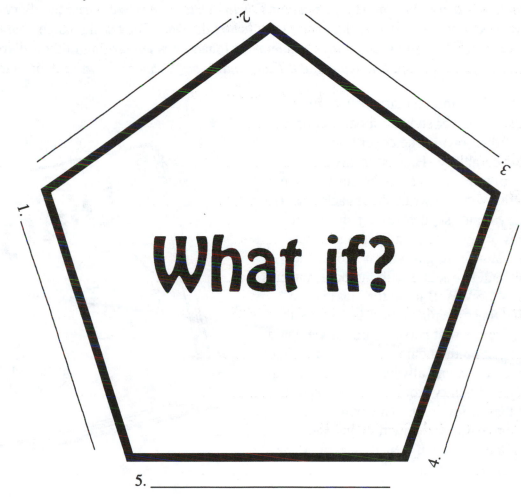

Now try one of these activities.

1. Use the ideas from your prediction pentagon to write a story about Sadako.

2. Make another pentagon and write predictions about your own life. Then, compare your pentagon with the one you made for Sadako. Write a description of how they are similar and how they are different.

3. Work with a group of six to eight students. Have the group members anonymously complete a prediction pentagon about themselves. After completing the pentagons, place them face down in a stack. Ask one group member to shuffle the stack. Redistribute the pentagons in random order. Have each group member read aloud a pentagon. Then try to guess who is being described by the information on each pentagon.

World War II Diary

A diary is a daily written account of what someone does, thinks, or feels.

Have each student keep a daily diary throughout the World War II Unit. The suggested daily diary topics on page 42 will help students view WW II from three different perspectives. Students write the diary entries, not from their own personal experiences and interpretations, but from the viewpoints of three different characters. When they are reading *V Is for Victory*, they will write the diary entries as if they are young Americans living on the home front during the war. They will change characters when reading *Number the Stars* and pretend to be Annemarie Johansen when writing in their diary. Then they will become Sadako from *Sadako and the Thousand Paper Cranes* and write their diary entries.

Students should construct a diary with a cover. They may use the cover shown on page 41 or design one of their own. The cover may be laminated for durability. Have students attach blank sheets of writing paper to the cover. Give them a different topic to write about each day. Use the daily diary topics suggested on page 42, or have students brainstorm a list of topics about which each character might write. The writing assignment should correlate with the book students are reading or the WW II topic the class is currently studying. Remind students to write their diary entries from a first person point of view as a young American on the home front, Annemarie, or Sadako. Students should always indicate at the top of each daily diary entry from which character's perspective they are writing. This will make it easier for them to analyze how the tone and impressions of events change as they assume the role of different characters.

Encourage students to record emotions and reactions that they believe their character would have displayed. Students may wish to include illustrations as part of their diary entries.

As a culminating writing activity, have students compare and contrast the three characters based on the diary entries. When examining similarities and differences have students ask themselves the following questions.

- What traits describe each character?
- How does each character feel about war and patriotism?
- How does each character react to the grim realities of war?
- How was the life of each character affected by the war?

WORLD WAR II DIARY

Look at the world through the eyes of American, Danish, and Japanese people.

Daily Diary Topics

V Is for Victory

Directions: Write your diary entry from the perspective of a young American on the home front during World War II.

Lesson One— I will always remember where I was when I heard the news about Pearl Harbor.

Lesson Two— President Franklin D. Roosevelt signed an order sending Japanese Americans to Relocation Camps. One of my classmates was sent away.

Lesson Three— Things have really changed at our house since my dad went to fight in the war and my mom went to work at the defense plant.

Lesson Four— My friends and I are doing all we can to help the war effort.

Lesson Five— Almost every house in the neighborhood has a blue star hanging in its window as a symbol of a loved one fighting in the war. My worst fear is...

Lesson Six— The wartime slogan, song, or poster that means the most to me is...

Lesson Seven— I wonder if life will ever be the way it was before World War II. Something that I know will never be the same is...

Number the Stars

Directions: Write your diary entry from Annemarie Johansen's perspective.

Lesson One — There are Nazi soldiers on every street corner. Their presence makes me feel...

Lesson Two— I am afraid for my friend, Ellen, because she is Jewish.

Lesson Three— We are not even safe in our own homes.

Lesson Four— I do not have a Great-aunt Birte. Why would Mama lie?

Lesson Five— I was never so frightened in my whole life as when the Nazis came to our prayer service for Great-aunt Birte.

Lesson Six— I know that someday I will see Ellen again.

Lesson Seven— Now I know what Uncle Henrik meant when he told me that it would be easier to be brave if I didn't know everything.

Lesson Eight— I have learned many hard lessons about life in the past two years.

Sadako and the Thousand Paper Cranes

Directions: Write your diary entry from Sadako Sasaki's perspective.

Lesson One— I have feelings of both sadness and happiness on Peace Day.

Lesson Two— I was not at war with the Americans. I cannot have the atom bomb disease!

Lesson Three— I believe with my whole heart that the golden crane can make me well.

Lesson Four— No matter what happens, I will always be part of my family.

Lesson Five— My wish for the world is...

There are many other topics that you may wish to assign as daily writing activities when studying World War II from the American perspective. Suggested topics include: how Americans viewed Adolf Hitler and the Nazi Party, the qualities of President Franklin D. Roosevelt or President Dwight D. Eisenhower, President Harry S. Truman's decision to use the atomic bomb, conscientious objectors, the aftermath of the war in Europe, the prosecution of war criminals, and post-war relations with the Soviet Union.

World War II Vocabulary

Use the following World War II vocabulary list as a resource for activities and discussions.

1. **Allies:** countries fighting with the United States against the Axis powers.
2. **atom bomb:** powerful weapon created from the splitting of atoms. It was used by President Harry S. Truman on the Japanese cities of Hiroshima and Nagasaki to end World War II.
3. **Axis powers:** the alliance of Germany, Italy, and Japan.
4. **"Big Three":** Stalin, Churchill, and Roosevelt. They worked together to defeat Germany.
5. **Sir Winston Churchill:** Prime Minister of Great Britain during the war.
6. **Concentration Camps:** prison camps established by Adolf Hitler and the Nazi Party for Jews and other political prisoners during the war.
7. **D-Day:** invasion of Normandy, France, by the Allies (June 6, 1944).
8. **Dictator:** a person who has complete power and authority over a country.
9. **Dwight D. Eisenhower:** supreme commander of the Allied forces during the war who later became the 34th president of the United States.
10. **Hiroshima:** Japanese city on which the first atomic bomb was dropped (August 6, 1945).
11. **Adolf Hitler:** dictator of Germany during the war.
12. **Holocaust:** mass murder of European Jews by Adolf Hitler and the Nazi Party.
13. **Home front:** term given to the United States mainland during the war.
14. **Jews:** people persecuted by Adolf Hitler and the Nazis because their religion was Judaism.
15. **Benito Mussolini:** dictator of Italy during the war.
16. **Nagasaki:** Japanese city on which the second atomic bomb was dropped (August 9, 1945).
17. **Nazis:** shortened name for the German political party called the National Socialist German Worker's Party and commanded by Adolf Hitler.
18. **Patriotic:** showing love and support for one's own country.
19. **Pearl Harbor:** American base in Hawaii that was bombed by Japanese planes on December 7, 1941. The bombing of Pearl Harbor forced the United States to enter the war.
20. **Ration:** to allow only certain amounts of food, gasoline, and other goods to each person.
21. **Relocation camps:** special camps in the United States where Japanese Americans were detained after the bombing of Pearl Harbor.
22. **Franklin D. Roosevelt:** 32nd president of the United States. He has been the only president who was elected four times, serving a total of twelve years.
23. **Rosie the Riveter:** symbol of American women who went to work in factories during the war. (A rivet is a small metal nail that joins two pieces of metal.)
24. **Joseph Stalin:** dictator of the Soviet Union from 1929 - 1953.
25. **Swastika:** emblem on the Nazi flag. The swastika was a cross with the ends bent at right angles.
26. **General Hideki Tojo:** military dictator who controlled Japan during the war.
27. **Harry S. Truman:** became the 33rd United States president after President Roosevelt died.
28. **Veteran:** soldier who returns home from war.
29. **V-E Day:** "Victory in Europe Day" when Germany surrendered (May 8, 1945).
30. **V-J Day:** "Victory in Japan" when Japan surrendered (September 2, 1945).
31. **War bonds:** certificates sold by the United States government to pay for the war.

Headline News

During World War II, Americans on the home front were desperate for news about the war. Almost every family had relatives serving overseas. Newspapers were a good source of war news. Throughout World War II, there were many momentous front page headlines from the bombing of Pearl Harbor to the surrender of the Japanese. Below is a list of some of the events from World War II about which students could write a front page news story.

Suggested Topics

Germany Invades Poland	Women Enter the Work Force
The United States Enters the War	President Franklin D. Roosevelt Dies
Japanese Americans Are Sent to Relocation Camps	Adolf Hitler Is Defeated
	War Criminals Are Prosecuted
Americans Use Rationing Coupons	D-Day
Harry S. Truman Becomes President	Nazi Concentration Camps
The Allies Discover the Horrors of Nazi Concentration Camps	V-E Day
	Japan Bombs Pearl Harbor
Atomic Bombs Are Used on Japan	Americans Are Asked to Tighten Their Belts
V-J Day	Churchill Claims Victory

Newspaper Activities

1. Discuss with students the components of a front page story. Using a daily newspaper, identify the headline, dateline, by-lines, captions, etc. Emphasize the importance of the lead sentence and lead paragraph. Help students discriminate between fact and opinion.

2. Have students work with a partner to research one of the events listed above. As students do their research, they should look for information that answers these questions: Who and what is the news story going to be about? Where and when did the event happen? How and why did the event happen? Have students write rough drafts of their news stories. When they are ready to publish their front page story, have them use a copy of the newspaper form on page 45. Remind students to include a picture and a caption.

   Arrange the stories in chronological order. You may wish to display them as a time line of World War II on a classroom bulletin board, or you may bind them in a book and have students share them at "The Spirit of America" Day (pages 68-69).

3. To extend this activity, turn your classroom into a newspaper publishing company. Have students pretend to be employees working on one of the following assignments: News Department, Business Section, Sports Section, Feature Stories, Entertainment Section, Editorial Section, Art and Photography, Advertising and Circulation, Layout and Printing, Editing and Publishing.

The class newspaper could focus on a specific time period, such as the week following the bombing of Pearl Harbor. Have students share copies of the class newspaper with their families.

Extra! Extra! Read All About It!

HEADLINE NEWS

Haiku Happenings

Haiku is a short Japanese verse which dates back to very early Japanese history. It may have developed from the five-line verse form called the tanka. The word "haiku" actually means game verse.

A haiku consists of 3 lines. The first line has five syllables, the second line has seven syllables, and the third line has five syllables. A haiku is usually written about a subject related to nature. The author of a haiku tries to use descriptive words that paint a picture in the mind of the reader.

Writing haiku in the classroom has become a popular activity in American classrooms. It is an excellent way to help students relate to Japanese literature and culture. When writing haiku, grammar and punctuation are not the main emphasis. Therefore, students are free to be creative and focus on the imagery created by their descriptions. Since nature is the main topic of haiku, this lesson could easily be extended across the curriculum to science activities. Provide students with the opportunity to illustrate their haiku.

Here are two examples of haiku.

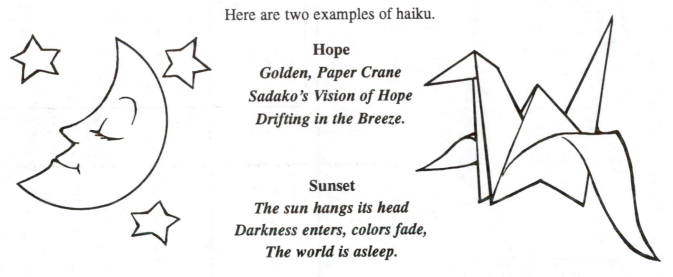

Hope
Golden, Paper Crane
Sadako's Vision of Hope
Drifting in the Breeze.

Sunset
The sun hangs its head
Darkness enters, colors fade,
The world is asleep.

First, ask students to choose a subject related to nature for their haiku. Then, draw the following organizer on the chalkboard or on a transparency. Have students use the organizer as a guide for writing their haiku. Point to the organizer as you remind students that a haiku consists of three lines that follow this pattern: five syllables in the first line, seven syllables in the second line, and five syllables in the third line.

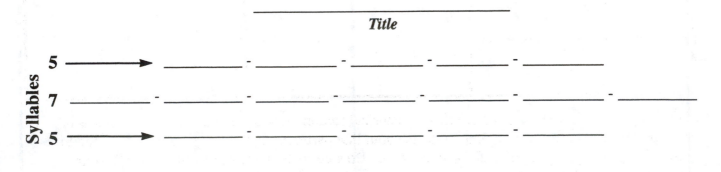

Title

Historical Fiction

Historical fiction is a story centered around actual historical facts and describes life in the past. Historical fiction contains facts as well as details that are imaginary, or made up. Analyze the two literature selections *Number the Stars* and *Sadako and the Thousand Paper Cranes*. Fill out the chart shown below to discriminate between events from the stories that are actual historical facts and those that are fictional.

Title of Book	Historical Facts	Fictional Events
Number the Stars		
Sadako and the Thousand Paper Cranes		

Now try your hand at writing a story that is historical fiction. Choose a period in history that is of interest to you. Do research to find out facts about that particular time period. Use a story map to plan your characters, setting, plot, goals, and outcome. Be sure to combine historical facts with your creative imagination.

Character Comparison

Character traits describe the unique qualities of a person. Annemarie in *Number the Stars* and Sadako in *Sadako and the Thousand Paper Cranes* each possesses very distinctive qualities. Using the list in the box, decide which traits best describe these characters and write them in their silhouettes shown below.

Character Traits

Daring	Lazy	Loving	Obedient
Respectful	Friendly	Pessimistic	Honest
Talkative	Conceited	Shy	Confident
Ambitious	Bold	Serious	Bossy
Proud	Energetic	Helpful	Courageous
Persistent	Compassionate	Generous	Cowardly
Adventurous	Intelligent	Mischievous	Trustworthy
Self-centered	Curious	Loyal	Fearful
Optimistic	Selfish	Brave	Humorous
Dishonest	Rude	Arrogant	Cheerful

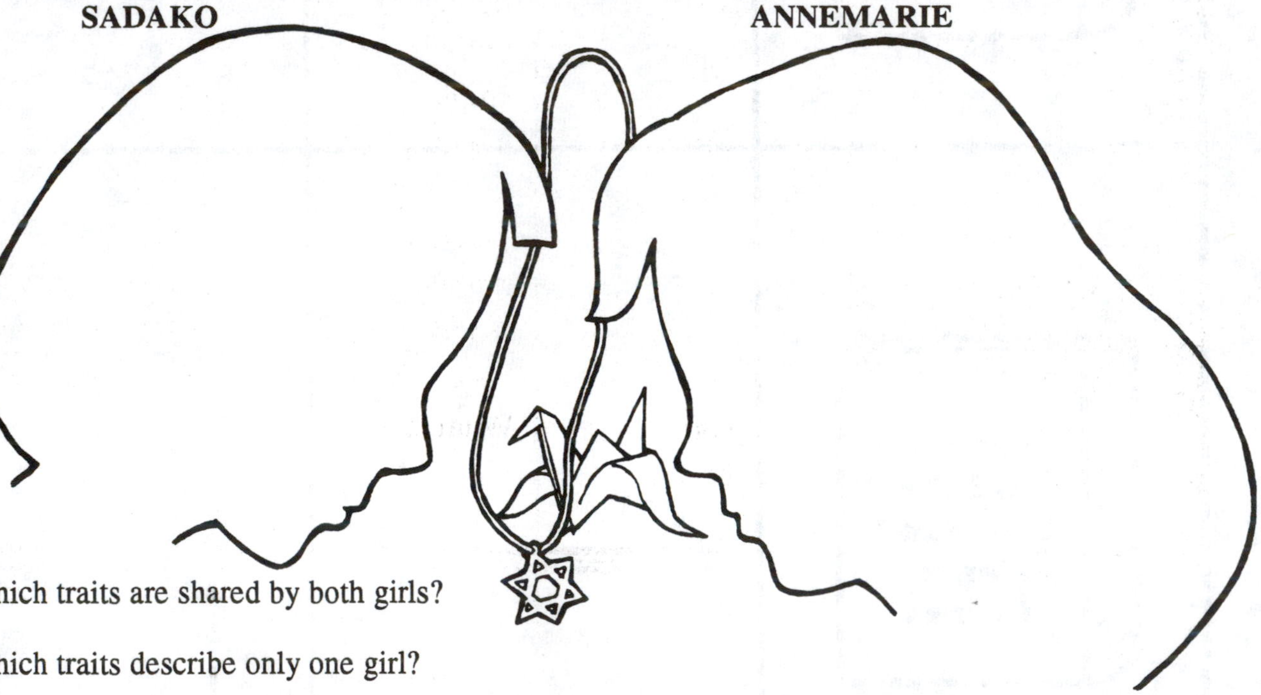

SADAKO   **ANNEMARIE**

1. Which traits are shared by both girls?

2. Which traits describe only one girl?

3. Give details from the story to support your choice of traits for both girls.

4. Are there any traits not in the list shown above that you think describe these girls? If there are, add them to the silhouettes.

5. Make a silhouette portrait of yourself. Identify traits in the list shown above that describe you. Write those traits on your silhouette.

Doing Without

"Use it up, Wear it out, Make it do, or Do Without."

During World War II, the needs of the soldier came before the needs of the consumer on the home front. To prevent prices from skyrocketing due to shortages of consumer goods, a governmental agency called the Office of Price Administration (OPA) did two things.

1. The OPA set price limits on many items.

2. The agency began rationing products such as sugar, coffee, gas, shoes, meat, fish, flour, and canned goods.

Under the OPA's system of rationing, each American was given ration coupons every month. These coupons were worth 48 Blue Points which could be used to buy processed foods, and 64 Red Points, which could be used to buy meat, butter, and fats. In addition to paying the price of an item, consumers also had to give up the required number of ration points.

The rationing schedules of the OPA were always changing as a result of supply and demand. To help consumers keep track of these changes, the OPA provided tables that gave an updated listing of food point values. Pages 50 and 51 contain information from the actual OPA rationing schedules for September, 1944. Have students use these schedules for the following activities. Remind students that they are only allowed 64 Red Points (meats, butter, fat) and 48 Blue Points (processed foods) per month!

Rationing Activities

1. Ask students how many total ration points were used to purchased the following items: 1 lb. (0.4536 kg) porterhouse steak, ½ lb. (226.8 g) of cheddar cheese, 10 oz. (300 g) canned apricots, 8 oz. (226.8 g) tomato juice, and 1 can of whole kernel corn. Ask how many of these points were red and how many were blue. Then ask how many ration points were left for the rest of the month.

2. Explain to students that consumers tried to purchase foods that did not require any ration points in order to make their points last an entire month. Have students list three items from each schedule that did not require points.

3. Have students plan a meal for their family. Ask them to figure out how many red points and blue points the meal would cost.

4. Plan how you would use your 64 Red Points and 48 Blue Points for an entire month. What foods would you buy that did not cost any points? (**Note:** Each person could automatically purchase 2 pounds (1000 g) of sugar per month without using ration points.)

5. Have students write word problems that can be solved using the Rationing Schedules.

6. Have students set up algebraic rationing equations for classmates to solve. For example:
   1 T-bone steak + 1 lb. (0.4536 kg) of shrimp = 8 oz. (226.8 g) container of applesauce + x.

Doing Without (*cont.*)

Rationing Schedule
Red Stamp Consumer Point Values, September, 1944
Meats, Fish, Fats, and Dairy Products

BEEF	Grades AA, A,B	LAMB	Grades AA, A,B	PORK	Points per lb. (453.6 g)	VEAL	Points per lb. (453.6 g)
Porterhouse Steak	14	Loin Chops	10	Tenderloin	8	Loin Chops	0
T-Bone Steak	13	Leg Chops and Steaks	8	Roast Loin	8	Shoulder Chops	0
Sirloin Steak	13	Sirloin Roast	7	Ham-Boneless	6	Rump Roast	0
Boneless Rump Roast	12	Shoulder Chops	5	Shoulder	0	Shoulder Roast	0
Short Ribs	0	Chuck Crosscut	3	Knuckles	0	Flank Meat	0
Hamburger-ground beef	0	Lamb Patties	0	Spareribs	0	Ground Veal and Patties	0

BACON	Points per lb. (453.6 g)	FISH	Points per lb. (453.6 g)	SAUSAGE	Points per lb. (453.6 g)	OTHER MEATS	Points per lb. (453.6 g)
Canadian	8	Shrimp	6	Dry	0	Luncheon Meats	0
Sides, aged dry-cured	2	Tuna	6	Semidry	0	Tamales	0
Sliced	0	Oysters	2	Fresh, Smoked	0	Meat Loaf	0

FATS, OILS, DAIRY	Points per lb. (453.6 g)	FATS, OILS, DAIRY	Points per lb. (453.6 g)	FATS, OILS, DAIRY	Points per lb. (453.6 g)	FATS, OILS, DAIRY	Points per lb. (453.6 g)
Creamery Butter	20	Margarine	2	Cheddar Cheese	12	Cottage Cheese	6
Country/Farm Butter	12	Shortening	0	Colby Cheese	12	Cream Spread	6
Process Butter	12	Salad/Cooking Oil	0	Creamed Cheese	6	Canned Milk	1

Doing Without *(cont.)*

Rationing Schedule

Blue Stamp Consumer Point Values, September, 1944,
Processed Foods

Over	0 oz (0 g)	7 oz (210 g)	10 oz (300 g)	14 oz (420 g)	1 lb. 2 oz (.5136 kg)	1 lb. 6 oz (.6336 kg)
CANNED or **BOTTLED** including	7 oz (210 g)	10 oz (300 g)	14 oz (420 g)	1 lb. 2 oz (.5136 kg)	1 lb. 6 oz (.6336 kg)	2 lb. (.9072 kg)
FRUITS Apples	10	20	20	30	40	60
Apricots	10	20	20	30	40	60
Fruit Cocktail	10	20	30	40	50	80
Peaches	10	20	30	40	50	80
JUICES Grape Juice	10	10	10	20	20	30
Orange Juice	0	0	0	0	0	0
Tomato Juice	10	10	10	20	20	30
VEGETABLES Corn (whole kernel)	0	0	0	0	0	0
Spinach	0	0	0	0	0	0
Tomatoes	10	10	10	20	20	30
SPREADS Jams, Preserves, Marmalades	0	0	0	0	0	0
Jellies	0	0	0	0	0	0
Fruit Butters	0	0	0	0	0	0
SPECIAL PRODUCTS Tomato Catsup	20	30	50	70	90	130
Tomato Sauce/Paste	0	0	0	0	0	0

51

The Manhattan Project and the Dawning of the Nuclear Age

Throughout the 1930's, scientists in the United States experimented with uranium and plutonium trying to discover the secrets of their atomic structure. In 1938, two scientists in Germany successfully split the nucleus of an atom. This became known as nuclear fission. President Franklin D. Roosevelt feared that Adolf Hitler would try to build a nuclear fission bomb. As a result, he secretly gave approval for a team of United States scientists to try and create the first atomic bomb.

The code name for this top secret project for unleashing the power of the atom was The Manhattan Project. The reason it was called this is because much of the early work was done in New York City. Three years later, on July 16, 1945, the first test explosion of an atomic bomb was conducted at Alamogordo Bombing Range in New Mexico. A short time later, the leaders for the Allies decided to use the atomic bomb on Japan.

The explosive power of the atomic bomb comes from the energy that is released when the nucleus of the atom is split, or broken apart. Basically, a particle called a neutron acts like a trigger by colliding with an atom and causing its nucleus to split. The splitting atom causes more neutrons to collide with other atoms causing them to split and creating a chain reaction. This chain reaction of splitting atoms is the source of the devastating explosive energy of the atomic bomb.

It is difficult to imagine the force of an atomic bomb. One megaton is the explosive force of one million tons of TNT. A ten-megaton atomic bomb would have the explosive power of ten million tons of TNT.

The Manhattan Project and the Dawning of the Nuclear Age *(cont.)*

The stages of an atomic bomb explosion are the initial blast, followed by a firestorm, and ending with the deadly radiation and fallout. When the fireball touches the Earth's surface, dust, dirt, and debris are sucked up, forming the mushroom cloud.

Following World War II, the United States built thousands of atomic bombs. The most powerful of these is the hydrogen bomb. Some hydrogen bombs have the explosive power of 65 million tons of TNT.

Radiation refers to energy that travels in waves and the transmission of atomic particles through space. Scientists have studied the thousands of people who survived the bombings of Hiroshima and Nagasaki. They have found strong links between the exposure to high amounts of radiation and the development of leukemia. Leukemia is a type of cancer in which a person's body makes too many white blood cells. Sometimes it is referred to as cancer of the blood. Leukemia used to be incurable. However, in recent years scientists have made remarkable progress in developing successful treatments.

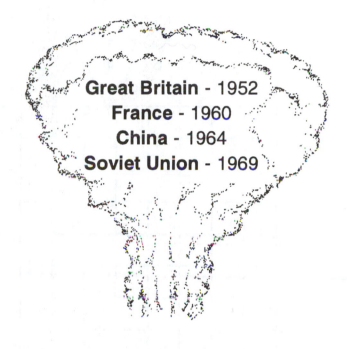

Great Britain - 1952
France - 1960
China - 1964
Soviet Union - 1969

In 1945, the United States was the only nation that had the atomic bomb. Other industrialized nations soon followed. The box below shows four of the countries that developed their nuclear capability after the United States.

In 1968, the United States, the Soviet Union, and Great Britain signed the Nuclear-Non Proliferation Treaty. This treaty set up strict requirements for countries that wanted to build a nuclear energy industry so that they would not develop nuclear weapons. However, it is believed that some of these countries have obtained nuclear weapons despite the treaty.

For Further Discussion and Research

1. Research to find out what progress has been made in recent years in arms control regulations.
2. Why has the decline of the Soviet Union been a major concern with regard to the regulation of their nuclear weapons?
3. The energy produced by nuclear fission has also been used in a constructive way. Nuclear energy is being used to produce electricity in many power plants around the world. Research to find out how nuclear energy is used to produce electricity. What are the pros and cons of using nuclear energy in power plants?
4. Do research to learn about other uses of nuclear energy.

Atom Bomb Wordsearch

Use the following words related to the atomic bomb to make a wordsearch in the grid shown below. The words may be written vertically, horizontally, or diagonally in the grid. Exchange your wordsearch with a classmate.

Manhattan Project	Nucleus
Hydrogen Bomb	Firestorm
Arms Control	Plutonium
Japan	Truman
Mushroom Cloud	Alamogordo
Radiation	Uranium
Megaton	Fallout
Neutrons	Nagasaki
Leukemia	Hiroshima
Fission	Chain Reaction

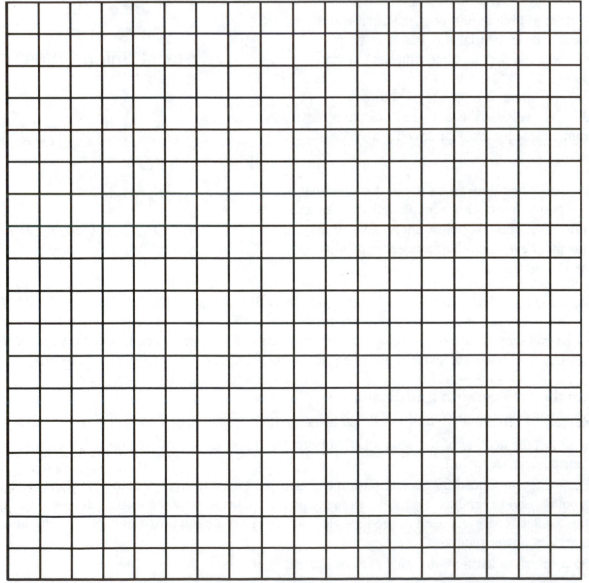

Difficult Decisions

Vice-President Harry S. Truman became president of the United States after President Franklin D. Roosevelt died in April, 1945. Shortly after becoming president, Truman was faced with the most difficult decision of his life. Should he use the newly invented atomic bomb against Japan in an effort to save American lives and end World War II?

Below is a list of key questions, arguments, and facts presented to President Truman. Any of the following formats may be used to address these issues: Classroom Discussion, Cooperative Learning Groups, Debate, Role-Playing or Dramatization.

For Discussion and Debate

1. The atomic bomb was such a new weapon that most people were not aware of the devastating effects it could produce. Consequently, some scientist believed that the United States should have conducted a public demonstration as a warning in an attempt to avoid actually using it.

2. President Truman was afraid that if a public test of this new weapon was unsuccessful, Japanese leaders would not take the United States seriously.

3. Many scientists felt the atomic bomb was too deadly and that there were too many questions about the extent of damage it would cause and what its long-lasting effects would be.

4. Some military advisors believed that Japan was already close to surrendering.

5. Other advisors believed that Japan still had a strong military. They feared that the war might last another two years and cause up to 500,000 more American casualties.

6. Should President Truman have warned the Japanese about the atomic bomb?

7. In July, 1945, President Truman warned the Japanese to surrender or be destroyed, but he did not tell them about the atomic bomb.

8. Scientists told President Truman that approximately 20,000 Japanese would die and many homes and factories would be destroyed if he used the atomic bomb.

9. In reality, the first atomic bomb killed 80,000 - 100,000 people and destroyed five square miles in Hiroshima. Three days later, the second atomic bomb killed 40,000 people in Nagasaki. Thousands more died later as a result of injuries and from exposure to radiation.

10. Japan surrendered on August 14th.

The development of the atomic bomb during World War II was the beginning of the nuclear weapons race. People began to worry that some day there would be a global nuclear war. Discuss how events of the Cold War added to the fear of a nuclear confrontation. How have more recent events increased or decreased the threat of nuclear war? How does the availability of nuclear weapons affect trouble spots around the world, such as the Middle East?

Time Line of World Events, 1933-1945

Use your knowledge of World War II and research skills to match the event with the correct date.

Event

_____ 1. General Montgomery leads the Allies to a victory over the Axis troops in North Africa.

_____ 2. The Germans take over Austria.

_____ 3. Adolf Hitler becomes the leader of Germany.

_____ 4. Japanese planes bomb the United States naval base at Pearl Harbor.

_____ 5. The Japanese attack China.

_____ 6. Germany surrenders (V-E Day) and Japan surrenders (V-J Day).

_____ 7. Japan takes over the Philippines.

_____ 8. Poland is invaded by German and Soviet troops.

_____ 9. The Allies send invasion forces to Normandy, France.

_____10. Franklin D. Roosevelt is re-elected as president of the United States for a third term.

Date

A. 1940

B. 1933

C. 1945

D. 1941

E. 1944

F. 1937

G. 1938

H. 1939

I. 1942

J. 1943

Now, use the dates and events that you matched above to construct a time line for World War II.

Time Line of World Events, 1933-1945

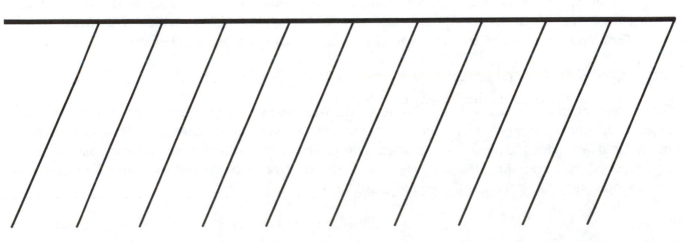

56

Heroes from the Home Front

Franklin D. Roosevelt

"...the only thing we have to fear is fear itself."

Harry S. Truman

"...The force from which the sun draws its power has been loosed upon those who brought war to the Far East."

Dwight D. Eisenhower

"We will accept nothing less than full Victory!"

The heroes shown above were presidents of the United States who played a major role during World War II, although not necessarily as president. Do research to learn more about one of these presidents. Use the information you find to complete the following outline.

_____

Name of Hero (Title)

I.   Early life

   A. _____

   B. _____

II. Education

   A. _____

   B. _____

III. Political or military career

   A. _____

   B. _____

   C. _____

   D. _____

IV. Noteworthy contributions or accomplishments

   A. _____

   B. _____

   C. _____

Use the completed outline to write a biography or prepare an oral report to present to the class.

Let's Play Ball!

During World War II, baseball games were a pastime that helped keep up morale of Americans on the home front. Use the words in the baseball diamond to fill in the blanks in the story shown below.

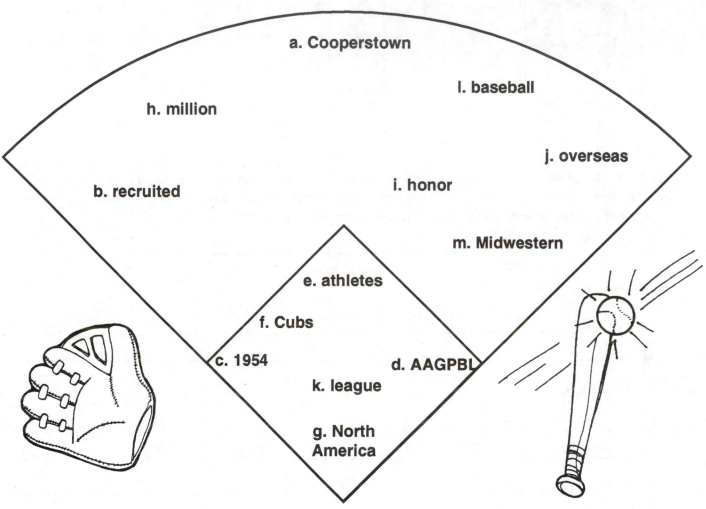

a. Cooperstown

l. baseball

h. million

j. overseas

b. recruited

i. honor

m. Midwestern

e. athletes

f. Cubs

c. 1954

d. AAGPBL

k. league

g. North America

During World War II, over half of the nation's major _1_____ baseball players joined the war effort and went to fight _2_____ . Phillip K. Wrigley, the owner of the Chicago _3_____ team, was afraid that Americans would lose interest in the game of _4_____ during the war years. He _5_____ the best female baseball players that he could find throughout the continent of _6_____ . He formed the All-American Girls Professional Baseball League, which was known by the letters _7_____ .

Each week, the female ballplayers were paid between $55 and $85. The AAGPBL existed in the _8_____ part of the United States for twelve years, from 1943 until _9_____ . This unique baseball league had teams in fourteen cities. During some seasons nearly one _10_____ fans enjoyed watching America's favorite pastime being played by some of the nation's top women _11_____ . Altogether, 550 women played in the AAGPBL. In 1988, the National Baseball Hall of Fame located in _12_____ , New York, added a special exhibit to _13_____ the AAGPBL and its players.

A Changing Germany

1. European Boundaries Before World War I (1914)

2. European Boundaries After World War I

3. European Boundaries After World War II

A Changing Germany *(cont.)*

4. European
   Boundaries
   Today

For Discussion and Research

1. Label and color Germany on the maps on pages 59 and 60. Use different colors to distinguish the difference between East Germany and West Germany on map #3, "European Boundaries After World War II." What can you conclude about the stability of Germany's borders since 1914?

2. Research and summarize the historical events that caused Germany's borders to change for each of the four maps.

3. What was the Berlin Wall, and what finally caused it to "tumble down"?

4. Germans are proud of their country and their rich heritage. Learn more about today's Germany by doing research. Gather information about one of the topics listed in the box shown below. Use this information to make a travel poster, a brochure, or a miniature book.

Government	People	Major Cities
Capital	Population	Economy
Climate	Language	Imports/Exports
Geography	Tourist Attractions	History
Education	Celebrations	Sports

A Patriotic Poster

Slogans, songs, and advertisements promoting patriotism were everywhere during World War II. Design your own poster in the space below that encourages patriotism and reflects the spirit of the American home front during World War II. Could your poster also be used to promote patriotism today?

Origami on Parade

Origami is the art of paper folding. Although it began in China, it flourished in Japan. In ancient days it was done by both the wealthy and poor. At one time, it was believed that paper contained spirits and could not be cut.

Experience this ancient art form. Follow the steps shown in the illustrations below to make an origami dog. Complete the head first and then the body. Slip the head on the top of the body.

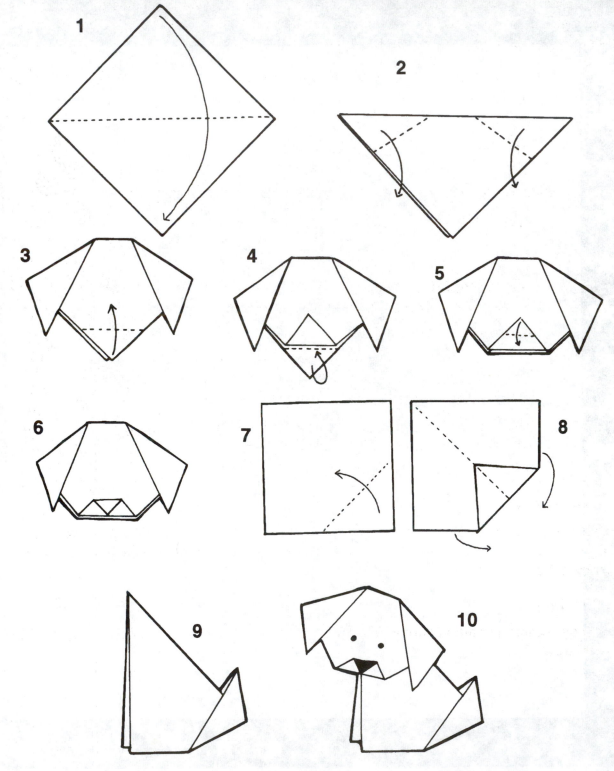

Exploring World War II through Music

In the aftermath of the attack on Pearl Harbor, the heroism of a navy chaplain was to be remembered forever in song. As this chaplain was setting up the altar for an outdoor Mass, his world was suddenly turned upside down by the onslaught of the Japanese attack. Instead of running for shelter, he ran for a machine gun, set it up on the altar, and began defending his base. The chaplain's bravery was remembered in the lyrics of this popular World War II song.

"Praise the Lord and Pass the Ammunition"
Praise the Lord and Pass the Ammunition
Praise the Lord and Pass the Ammunition
And We'll All Stay Free!

Another popular World War II song was "When the Lights Go On Again."

"When The Lights Go On Again"

When the lights go on again all over the world
And the boys are home again all over the world
And rain or snow is all that may fall from the skies above,
A kiss won't mean good-bye, but hello to love.

When the lights go on again all over the world
And the ships will sail again all over the world
Then we'll have time for things, like wedding rings,
And free hearts will sing,
When the lights go on again all over the world.

For Discussion

Analyze the lyrics of the songs shown above and the titles of other songs on page 64 that were popular during the World War II era. What can you conclude about the feelings, mood, or attitudes of many Americans during this time?

Trivia Time

What song became a tradition during World War II for the beginning of ball games played in the United States?

Exploring World War II Through Music *(cont.)*

Titles of Songs Popular During World War II

"I'll Get By"
"Accentuate the Positive"
"Comin' In on a Wing and a Prayer"
"Swinging on a Star"
"I'll Be Seeing You"
"To Each His Own"
"Don't Get Around Much Any More"
"Praise the Lord and Pass the Ammunition"
"The White Cliffs of Dover"
"Jingle, Jangle, Jingle"
"Boogie Woogie Bugle Boy"
"Shoo Shoo Baby"
"I Don't Want to Set the World on Fire"
"You'll Never Know"
"It's Been a Long, Long Time"
"Dance with a Dolly"
"Oh! What It Seemed to Be"
"Sentimental Journey"
'My Dreams Are Getting Better All the Time"
"Pistol Packin' Mama"
"Somebody Else is Taking My Place"
"Don't Sit Under the Apple Tree"
"Daddy"
"Chattanooga Choo-Choo"
"I Left My Heart at the Stage Door Canteen"
"When the Lights Go on Again"
"I'll Never Smile Again"

Compose your own lyrics for a song centering around a theme of world peace or patriotism. Your lyrics can be set to a familiar tune or performed as a rap.

The Sad Mistake: Japanese Relocation

A familiar saying, "hindsight is better than foresight," seems to apply to the plight of the Japanese Americans living on the west coast of the United States after the bombing of Pearl Harbor. Americans started to fear that Japan would attack the west coast next. They worried that Japanese Americans living on the west coast would feel allegiance to Japan and attack the United States from the inside. Feelings of anger, distrust, and fear were soon directed at all Japanese Americans living in the United States.

On February 19, 1942, President Franklin D. Roosevelt signed Executive Order 9066 forcing approximately 112,000 Japanese Americans who were living on the west coast into relocation camps. They had to sell their homes and businesses. Although the people being sent to the relocation camps were of Japanese descent, most of them were American citizens and many had relatives serving in the United States Army or Navy. An army unit of Japanese Americans, the 442 Regimental Combat Team, became one of the most famous units in the United States Army. Despite their loyalty to the United States, Japanese Americans continued to be treated unfairly.

Today, most Americans agree that the issue of relocation of Japanese Americans is a "blot" on the war record of the United States. In 1988, the Congress of the United States issued an official apology to the survivors of the Japanese-American relocation camps. Congress awarded these victims $1.25 billion in compensation payments.

Voice Your Opinion

Pretend that you are living on the west coast when Japan attacks Pearl Harbor. Pick one of the following writing assignments. Use facts to support your opinion.

1. Write a newspaper editorial supporting or opposing the use of relocation camps.

2. Write a letter to President Roosevelt supporting or opposing the use of relocation camps.

For Further Discussion

1. What alternatives to Japanese-American relocation camps do you think President Roosevelt should have tried?

2. Can you identify other times in history when fear and hatred have led to the unfair treatment of a specific group of people? Is there any place in the world where this is now occurring?

3. What can your generation do to continue the fight against bigotry and prejudice?

Recycling, Then and Now

Most people agree that the concept of recycling first became popular during World War II. When the United States entered the war, international trade was suspended. Raw materials were needed to manufacture tanks, airplanes, battleships, and ammunition. Americans on the home front began collecting tin foil, cans, scrap metal, glass, paper, rubber, and even nylon stockings so that these materials could be recycled and used for the war effort. People even recycled fat to be used in nitroglycerine for bombs. Recycling became the patriotic thing to do.

When the war ended, most Americans felt that there was no longer a need to conserve or recycle. Today, people realize that the "throw away" attitude has resulted in an enormous environmental problem. Garbage dumps and sanitary landfills cannot cope with the approximately 160 million tons of solid waste thrown out by Americans every year. The idea of recycling has once again become popular across the nation. People are collecting materials, such as glass, aluminum, metal, paper, and plastic, and taking them to local recycling centers.

Recycling Activities for the Classroom

1. Make a classroom bulletin board for students to display items that can be recycled, ideas for recycling, and current events articles about recycling. Title your bulletin board "RECYCLING — It's in the News" (page 74).

2. Hold a contest to see who can come up with the most creative way to reuse a container that has been thrown away. Students can use containers, such as milk cartons, 2-liter soda bottles, plastic shopping bags, aluminum cans, and cardboard boxes. Be sure students thoroughly clean the containers before they begin working on their project for the contest.

3. Have students write letters to persuade their families or a friends to start recycling. Tell them to be sure to explain why they think recycling is important. Have them do research about recycling so they can include specific facts that support their opinions.

4. Art Projects
    *   Have students make posters to place in your community that encourage everyone to recycle.
    *   Ask students to decorate used paper grocery bags with ideas about recycling. Give the decorated bags to your local grocery store for reuse.
    *   Have students try to make their own recycled paper.

5. Conduct an experiment by burying various types of garbage in a planter filled with a moderate amount of dirt. Suggested types of garbage include pieces of newspaper, wood, aluminum foil, plastic wrap, tissue, fabric, cardboard, fruit, and vegetables. After burying the objects, put the planter in a place where it can receive plenty of sunlight and be sure students water it regularly. Explain that the purpose of both of these actions is to duplicate outside conditions. Periodically, have students unearth the objects to check their state of decomposition. Ask students to draw conclusions based on their observations.

Recycling, Then and Now *(cont.)*

6. Divide the class into cooperative learning groups. Have students do research to find out what happens to materials once they reach the recycling center. Have them make a diagram to show the recycling process.

7. Invite a guest speaker from a local recycling center to visit with your class.

8. Take a field trip to a local recycling center.

9. Recycle used clothing or toys that are still in good shape by having a collection drive and donating the items to a local charity.

10. Duplicate the address card shown below as many times as necessary. Have students use a telephone directory to find out where some local recycling centers are located. Ask them to fill out the cards with the appropriate information. If a map of your community is available, help students locate and mark the recycling centers on the map. Before marking the map, students may need to call the centers to ask for the names of nearby intersections. Then have students write a business letter to one of the recycling centers for which they have made an address card. In the letters, students should request information about how the recycling center operates and an explanation of any new methods that the center has for handling America's garbage and waste disposal problem. Students may wish to ask for suggestions on how your school and community can help in the effort. If your community has a small number of recycling centers, this activity can be worked on by cooperative learning groups or with the entire class.

Name of Business_____

Address: _____

Area Code: ____ Phone Number: _____

Type of Business _____

Celebrating "The Spirit of America" Day

As a culminating activity, announce that your class will have a special celebration called "The Spirit of America" Day. The following activities can easily be adapted to meet the individual needs of your students and to accommodate for the availability of resources in your school and community. Choose from these ideas or have students brainstorm a list of activities they feel promote patriotism and a sense of pride in America.

1. Send an invitation (page 69) to any guests (other classes, school administrators, parents, community members, etc.) you would like to invite to "The Spirit of America" Day.

2. Use this day as an opportunity to honor local veterans. You may wish to have these activities on Veterans' Day. Invite veterans to be guest speakers and to share memorabilia such as pictures, newspaper clippings, maps, and uniforms.

3. Have students design posters to display around the school that promote patriotism, world peace, and cooperation among the peoples of the world (page 61).

4. Invite students' relatives to speak to the class about their World War II experiences.

5. Have students read the Class Big Book, "The Long Road to Peace" (pages 70-71); their research papers, "Heroes From the Home Front" (page 57); and selections from their daily diary entries (pages 40-42).

6. Ask for volunteers to perform the songs that were popular during World War II (pages 63-64, Bibliography) or the songs they wrote for promoting world peace or patriotism (page 64).

7. Invite everyone in the school to wear red, white, and blue to show their pride in America. Organize a short parade with flags and patriotic music.

8. Ask students to share what they have learned about the German and Japanese cultures. Have them report on how Germany has changed during this century (pages 59-60). Allow them to display their origami projects (pages 37, 62, 74) and read aloud their haiku (pages 46, 74).

9. Have participants of "The Spirit of America" Day trace and cut out patterns of their hands to spell out the words "PEACE" or "AMERICA" for a bulletin board (page 73).

10. Make copies of the badge on page 69 for students to cut out, color, and wear.

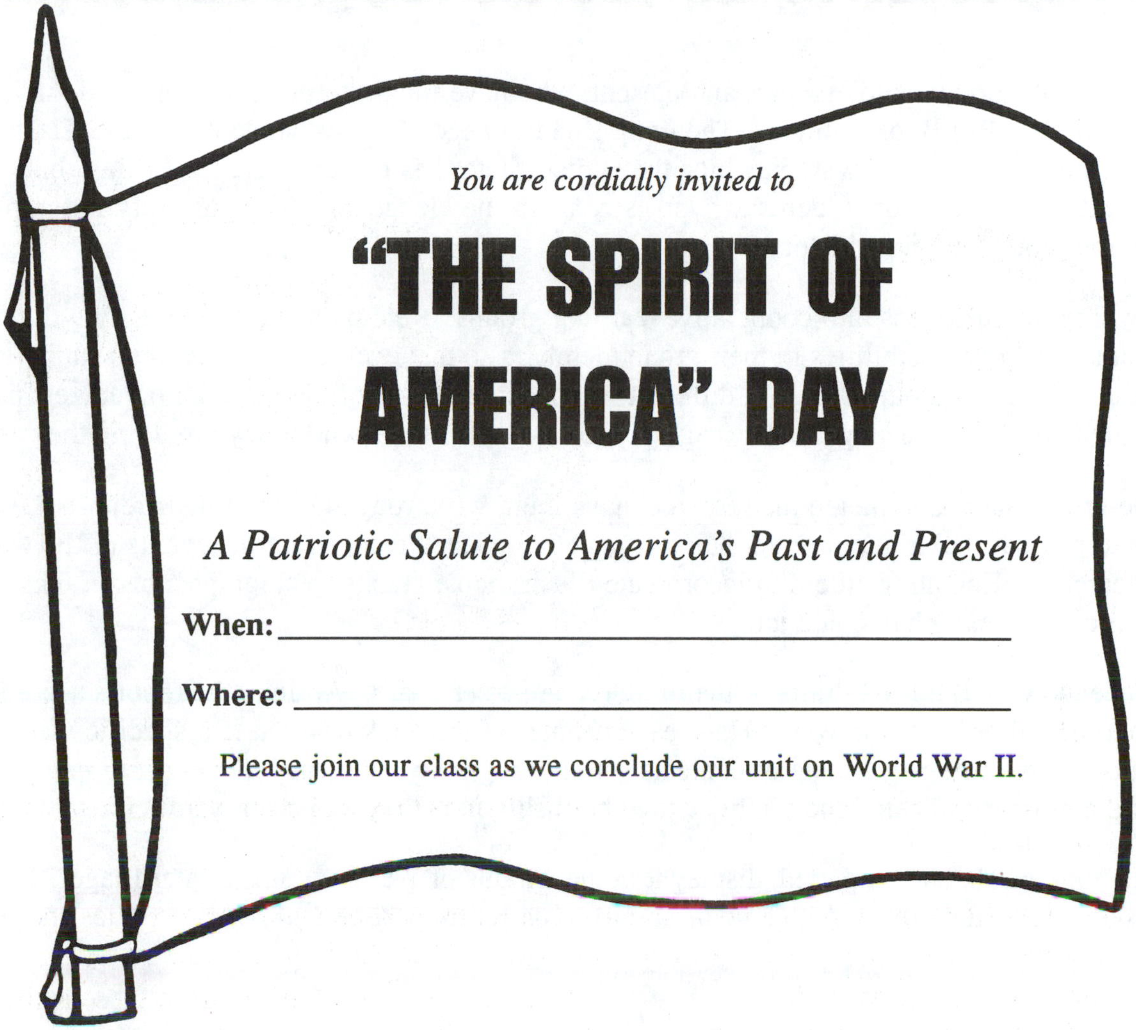

You are cordially invited to

"THE SPIRIT OF AMERICA" DAY

A Patriotic Salute to America's Past and Present

When: _____

Where: _____

Please join our class as we conclude our unit on World War II.

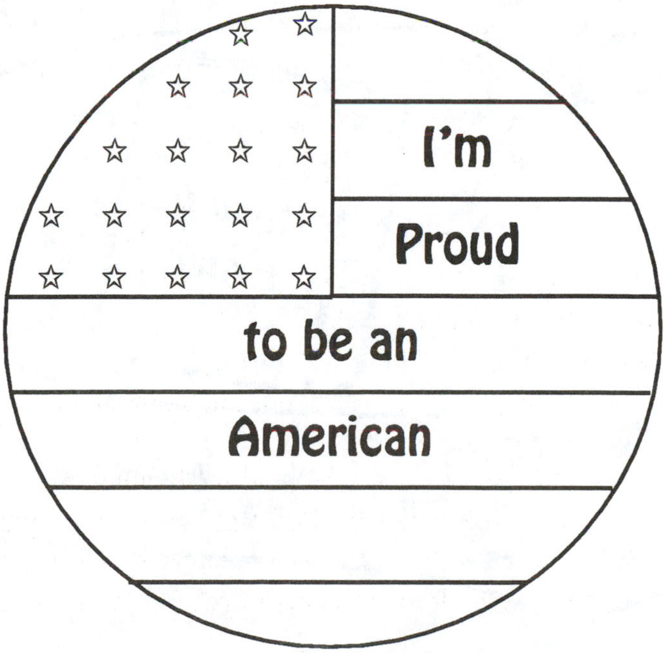

I'm

Proud

to be an

American

Writing a Class Big Book

As a salute to American soldiers, past and present, who have fought to preserve our freedom, have your class write a Big Book entitled, "The Long Road to Peace." Have students use the Class Big Book to tell about the major wars in which the United States has been involved. Writing this book is an excellent opportunity for students to synthesize their knowledge about the concepts and implications of war throughout American history.

Begin by dividing the class into cooperative learning groups. Remind students that they will need to assign individual responsibilities to their group members so that everyone has the opportunity to participate. Have the groups research different wars. Place copies of the research organizer (page 71) in the Clouds of War Learning Center (page 72) for students to use while they are doing their research.

After the groups have completed the research, have them write rough drafts of their reports. Ask students to pay particular attention to their writing style as they reconstruct the events of the war they have researched. Encourage them to incorporate illustrations, graphs (pictographs, bar graphs, line graphs, circle graphs), charts, and tables.

Have students write the final drafts of their reports on poster board. Arrange the reports according to the chronological order of the wars. Have each chapter of the book devoted to a specific war. Have volunteers make a title page, table of contents, and bibliography. You may also wish to include an index and a glossary. Then, bind the book together using metal rings or thick yarn.

After the book has been completed, display it in the Clouds of War Learning Center (page 72). You may wish to have students read it aloud as part of "The Spirit of America" Day activities (page 68).

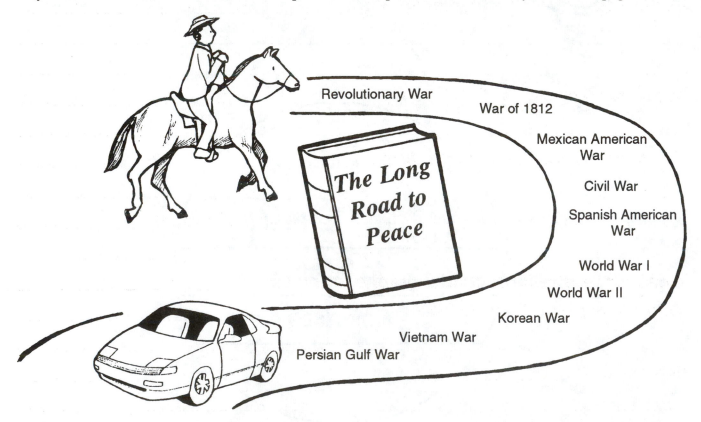

The Long Road to Peace

Use this form to help organize the information you obtain when researching a war in United States history for the Class Big Book entitled, *The Long Road to Peace*.

War: _____

Dates: _____

Parties or countries involved: _____

Reasons leading to the conflict: _____

_____

_____

Casualties/Destruction: _____

_____

_____

Outcome or results of the war: _____

_____

_____

Terms of treaty, surrender, or withdrawal: _____

_____

_____

Major battles: _____

_____

Outstanding leaders during the war: _____

_____

Postwar relations or long term effects on the United States: _____

_____

Ideas for illustrations, charts, graphs, or maps: _____

Other interesting facts or information: _____

_____

Sources: _____

_____

Clouds of War Learning Center

The Clouds of War Learning Center may be set up as a bulletin board with a table in front of it or with a cardboard display on a large table. Make the learning center title by cutting three clouds out of poster board and writing "CLOUDS OF WAR" on the clouds, one word per cloud. Create a three-dimensional effect by gluing cotton balls or quilt batting around the words on the clouds. Use string or yarn to hang the clouds from the ceiling. Place a world map on the center section of the display. Students will use the map to locate the countries involved in the wars being researched. Color-coded push pins should be used to mark specific countries on the map. On the left side of the display, provide copies of "The Long Road to Peace" organizational form (page 71). On the right side of the display, list the names of the wars being researched by your class.

The table in this center gives students a place to display the projects they complete during this unit. Other resources and books related to World War II may also be placed on the table. Students may wish to display some of their relatives' WW II memorabilia, such as photos, maps, newspaper clippings, and uniforms. Additional tables may be needed if veterans who are invited to "The Spirit of America" Day bring additional materials to display. They may wish to bring items from other wars, such as the Vietnam War or the Persian Gulf War. The ideas for this learning center may be easily adapted to meet the individual needs of your classroom.

Bulletin Boards

This bulletin board has a powerful message and is extremely easy to construct. Cover the background with butcher paper or try using aluminum foil if you would like to create a striking effect. Cut apart a large world map or picture of a globe so that it looks like pieces of a jigsaw puzzle. Then, place the map or picture on the bulletin board, piecing it back together. To make the border, distribute red, white, and blue construction paper to the participants in "The Spirit of America" Day (page 68). Have the participants use this paper to trace and cut out hand prints. **Alternative:** To make another quick, easy, and effective bulletin board, use the red, white, and blue hand prints to spell out "PEACE" or "AMERICA."

Use this bulletin board for students to display their interpretations of how Americans on the home front contributed to the war effort. Cover the background with butcher paper, construction paper, or tissue paper. To obtain a three-dimensional effect, use yarn or string and push pins to make the lines of latitude and longitude. Place an outline map of the United States over the yarn or string. Attach a small U.S. flag near the top of the map. Have students make small posters that tell about how the war affected the home front. Possible topics include: Doing Without; Patriotism; Victory Gardens; Gasoline Rationing; Recycling; Songs, Slogans, and Posters; Food Rationing; and Rosie the Riveter. Arrange the posters on the bulletin board.

Bulletin Boards (cont.)

The bulletin board shown above features Japan. It is used to display the haiku and origami projects students have completed during this unit. You may wish to include a map and flag of Japan. Use the colors of the Japanese flag (white and red) for the bulletin board by covering the background with white butcher paper and using red letters for the words. For "HAIKU HAPPENINGS," have students neatly copy their haiku on poster board or construction paper and draw illustrations for the borders. Then display them on the board. For "ORIGAMI ON PARADE," fold strips of red construction paper accordion style to make the letters for "ORIGAMI." Then, display the origami projects students have made.

This is a very quick and easy bulletin board with a high level of student participation. Use empty cereal boxes to cut out letters for the word "RECYCLING." Then, use old newspapers to cut out letters for the phrase "IT'S IN THE NEWS." Ask students to bring in examples of recyclable materials so that you can attach them to the board. You may wish to have students classify the bulletin board into categories, such as plastic, cardboard, aluminum, and paper.

Make a Pamphlet

Have students make pamphlets that tell about *V Is for Victory, Number the Stars*, and *Sadako and the Thousand Paper Cranes*. They can work on a pamphlet as they are reading or after completing each book. Have students begin a pamphlet by folding a piece of white construction paper into thirds, accordion style. Then use the following suggestions to help them organize each pamphlet.

Suggestions for *V Is for Victory* are above the dotted lines. Suggestions for *Number the Stars* and *Sadako and the Thousand Paper Cranes* are below the dotted lines.

(Front Cover) Students should include: • cover art • the title of the book • the author of the book • the author of the pamphlet • the illustrator of the pamphlet • today's date · · · · · · · · · · · · · · Same suggestions as shown above.	**"Bombs Bring War Home"** • Students should tell about the main ideas in this chapter. They may include illustrations throughout. · · · · · · · · · · · · · · **Major Characters** Students should include: • a physical description (if provided) • a description of their character traits Students may include: • illustrations throughout	**"The Home Front Goes to Work" and "America Tightens Its Belt"** • Students should tell about the main ideas in these chapters. · · · · · · · · · · · · · · **Setting** Students should include: • a map showing where the story takes place • a description of the location and time period
"Long Time No See" • Students should tell about the main ideas in this chapter. · · · · · · · · · · · · · · **Plot** Students should include: • a sequenced description of the major story events • a description of major goals or problems that occur • a description of obstacles that interfere with goals or complicate problems	**"A Country United and Divided"** • Students should tell about the main ideas in this chapter. · · · · · · · · · · · · · · **Conclusion** Students should include: • a description of how the story ends • an explanation describing why the goals were or were not reached or why the problems were or were not resolved	**"The American Century Dawns"** • Students should tell about the main ideas in this chapter and give their recommendations. · · · · · · · · · · · · · · **Recommendations** Students should include: • an explanation of why they would or would not recommend the book to other students • a few specific examples of things they did or did not enjoy about the book

Dear Parents,

Our class is beginning to study a unit about World War II. We will be using three highly recommended books (*V Is for Victory, Number the Stars, Sadako and the Thousand Paper Cranes*) to help students understand the complex issues of the war from different perspectives. In addition to studying how the war affected Americans living on the home front, our class will also look at World War II through the eyes of Jewish families living in Denmark and Japanese families living in Hiroshima, Japan. We will investigate the tragedies and hardships of the war, such as the bombing of Pearl Harbor, rationing, the Holocaust, and the use of the atomic bomb.

Students will be completing a variety of activities related to World War II. These activities integrate several subject areas, including art, math, science, social studies, language arts, music, and life skills.

We would like to invite some guest speakers to our class. Please notify us if you or someone you know would like to share a first-hand account of fighting in the war or what it was like to live on the home front during the war.

We are setting up a learning center called the "Clouds of War" in one area of our classroom. The center will be filled with resources and books related to World War II, as well as the projects completed by our class. We will also have space set aside for any materials that students bring from home. If you or any relatives have items related to World War II (photos, books, newspaper articles, maps, uniforms, memorabilia, etc.) that could be placed in our learning center, they would be greatly appreciated.

Thank you for helping to make this World War II Unit a successful and valuable learning experience for our class.

Sincerely,

Portfolio Assessment Form

Reading Student Conference

Student's Name: _____ Date: _____

Which of the three books did you enjoy most and why? _____

Would you like to read another book about World War II? _____

Why or why not? _____

_____

Writing Student Conference

Student's Name: _____ Date: _____

Which of the following writing activities for this unit did you complete? Which was your best piece of writing? Which writing activity did you enjoy the least? On which writing activity would you like to spend more time?

Anecdotal Notes

Student's Name: _____ Date: _____

Which group activities did this student participate in during the World War II unit._____

_____

Behavior Observed: _____

Which individual activities did this student participate in during the World War II unit?

_____

Behavior Observed: _____

Teacher's comments about the student's overall performance during this unit:

Bibliography

Fiction

Ackerman, Karen. *When Mama Retires*. Knopf, 1992.

Bauer, Marion Dane. *Rain of Fire*. Houghton Mifflin, 1983.

Bawden, Nina. *Henry*. Lothrup, 1988.

Bishop, Clarie Huchet. *Twenty and Ten*. Peter Smith, 1984.

Burke, Kathleen. "Winning the hearts and mind of an American facing war." *Smithsonian*. March, 1994: 66-69

Cooper, Susan. *Dawn of Fear*. Macmillan, 1989.

DeJong, Meindert. *The House of Sixty Fathers*. Harper, 1987.

Garrigue, Sheila. *The Eternal Spring of Mr. Ito*. Bradbury, 1985.

Green, Connie Jordan. *The War at Home*. Macmillan, 1989.

Hahn, Mary D. *Stepping on the Cracks*. Clarion, 1991.

Hartling, Peter. *Crutches*. Lothrup, 1988.

Holm, Anne. *North to Freedom*. Peter Smith, 1984.

Kerr, Judith. *When Hitler Stole Pink Rabbit*. Putnam, 1972.

Kogawa, Joy. *Naomi's Road*. Oxford, 1988.

Levitin, Sonia. *Journey to America*. Macmillan, 1986.

Lingard, Joan. *Tug of War*. Lodestar, 1990.

McSwigan, Marie. *Snow Treasure*. Scholastic, 1986.

Pearson, Kit. *The Sky Is Falling*. Viking Penguin, 1990.

Serraillier, Ian. *Escape from Warsaw* (original title: *The Silver Sword*). Scholastic, 1990.

Uchida, Yoshiko. *Journey to Topaz*. Creative Arts, 1985.

Vander Els, Betty. *The Bombers' Moon*. Farrar, 1984.

Westall, Robert. *The Machine Gunners*. McKay, 1990.

Yolen, Jane. *The Devil's Arithmetic*. Penguin, 1990.

Nonfiction

Adler, David. *We Remember the Holocaust*. Holt, 1989.

Bliven, Bruce. *The Story of D-Day*. Random House, 1981.

Chaikin, Miriam. *Friends Forever*. Harper, 1988.

Frank, Anne. *Anne Frank: The Diary of a Young Girl*. ABC-CLIO, 1989.

Graff, Stewart. *The Story of World War II*. Dutton, 1978.

Maruki, Toshi. *Hiroshima No Pika*. Lothrup, 1982.

Meltzer, Milton. *Rescue: The Story of How Gentiles Saved Jews in the Holocaust*. Harper, 1988.

Reiss, Johanna. *The Upstairs Room*. Harper, 1987.

Rossel, Seymour. *The Holocaust: The Fire That Raged*. Watts, 1989.

Snyder, Louis L. *World War II*. Watts, 1981.

Stefoff, Rebecca. *Recycling*. Chelsea House, 1991.

Stevenson, James. *Don't You Know There's A War On?* Greenwillow Books, 1992.

Cassette Tapes

Stage Door Canteen. A 3-cassette tape collection of 44 original World War II songs performed by the original artists. Available from JC Penney's Heartland Music Collection.

Teacher Created Materials, Inc.

233 *Peace*

314 *Literature and Critical Thinking - Historical Fiction*

343 *Connecting Geography and Literature*

424 *Number the Stars Literature Unit*

430 *Journey to Topaz Literature Unit*

481 *World History Simulations*

600 *A Trip Around the World*

906 *Newspaper and Reporting Set*

Answer Key

Page 11

1. the island of Oahu; the city of Honolulu
2. Pearl Harbor Naval Base was the center of command in the Pacific for the U.S. Navy. It is one of the world's largest and best sheltered naval anchorages.
3. Admiral Husband E. Kimmel
4. about 3,700 human casualties, 18 ships sunk or damaged, almost 200 planes destroyed
5. The memorial is built directly above the submerged battleship U.S.S. Arizona in Pearl Harbor. It commemorates the more than 1,000 men who were entombed in the battleship during the surprise attack by the Japanese on December 7, 1941.

6-8. Answers will vary.

Page 12

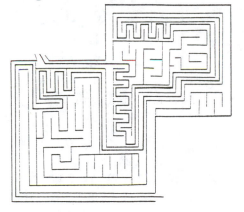

Page 13

1. Allied countries
2. Germany; Soviet Union
3. 3; 3
4. 76,000
5. 2,281,000

Page 15

Suggested answers include:

1. Japan surrendered.
2. Veterans needed scholarship help adjusting to life after the war and getting a fresh start.
3. Factories laid off many workers.
4. Factories gave returning veterans their old jobs as well as any new jobs.
5. The arms race, with the threat of nuclear war, began between the Soviet Union and the U.S.
6. Many couples married following the war and moved into homes of their own.
7. The women's liberation movement had its start following World War II.
8. The U.S. wanted to help rebuild war-torn Europe.
9. The Soviet-controlled zone of Germany became known as East Germany; the Allies granted its zones full independence, forming the country of West Germany.

Extending Cause-and-Effect

Examples include: certain antibiotics, sulfa drugs, DDT, nuclear power and weapons (atomic bomb 1945), nuclear reactor (1942), automatic digital computer (1944), xerography (1942), TVs and air conditioners became available to the general public and Tupperware (1945).

Page 16

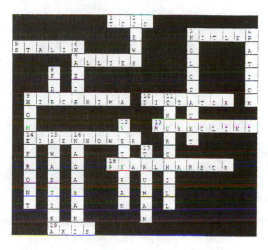

Page 27

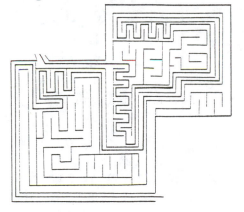

Answer Key *(cont.)*

Page 33

1. child
2. school
3. telephone
4. please
5. Good night!

Page 35

1943— Sadako was born.

Aug. 6, 1945— Atom bomb was dropped on Hiroshima.

Aug. 6, 1954— Sadako attended Hiroshima Peace Day celebration.

Autumn, 1954— Sadako first showed symptoms of leukemia.

Feb., 1955— Sadako first entered the Red Cross Hospital.

June, 1955— Sadako's class sent her a kokeshi doll.

July, 1955— Sadako went home for a visit to celebrate the O Bon holiday.

Oct. 25, 1955— Sadako died.

1958— Sadako's statues is unveiled in Hiroshima Peace Pa

Page 36

1. Last Monday in May
2. Decoration Day

3. Honor all Americans who have given their lives for their country.
4. Civil War
5. 1971
6. Answers should include three of the following: Flowers and flags are placed on the graves of those who have died in wars and other endeavors; military units, and other organizations take part in parades and programs; memorials are often dedicated and ceremonies are held at the grave of the Unknown Soldier at the Arlington National Cemetery in Virginia and at Gettysburg National Park; some ports set afloat tiny ships filled with flowers to honor those who have died at sea.
7. Since the end of World War I, volunteers have sold small red artificial poppies to raise money to help disabled veterans.
8. Answers should include four of the following: Mississippi - Last Monday in April; Alabama - Fourth Monday in April; Georgia - April 26; North and South Carolina - May 10; Virginia - Last Monday in May; Kentucky, Tennessee, Louisiana - June 3; and

Page 49

1. 1 lb. (0.4536 kg) porterhouse steak, 14 points
   ½ lb. (226.8 g) of cheddar cheese, 6 points
   10 oz. (300 g) canned apricots, 20 points
   8 oz. (226.8 g) tomato juice 10 points
   1 can of whole kernel corn 0 points
   Total points used = 50
   Number of red points = 20
   Number of blue points = 30
   Total ration points left for the month = 62

2-6. Accept appropriate responses.

Page 56

1. J	6. C
2. G	7. I
3. B	8. H
4. D	9. E
5. F	10. A

Page 58

1. K	8. M
2. J	9. C
3. F	10. H
4. L	11. E
5. B	12. A
6. G	13. I
7. D	

Page 63

The tradition of playing the Star-Spangled Banner before U.S. ball games began during WW II.

©1994 Teacher Created Materials, Inc.